Total career management

THE HENLEY MANAGEMENT SERIES

Series Adviser: Professor Bernard Taylor

Total career management
Strategies for creating management careers

Frances A. Clark

McGRAW-HILL BOOK COMPANY

London · New York · St Louis · San Francisco · Auckland
Bogotá · Caracas · Hamburg · Lisbon · Madrid · Mexico · Milan
Montreal · New Delhi · Panama · Paris · San Juan · São Paulo
Singapore · Sydney · Tokyo · Toronto

Published by
McGRAW-HILL Book Company Europe
Shoppenhangers Road, Maidenhead, Berkshire, SL6 2QL, England
Telephone 0628 23432
Fax 0628 770224

British Library Cataloguing in Publication Data

Clark, Frances A.
  Total career management: strategies for creating
  management careers. – (Henley management series)
  I. Title II. Series
  331.702
ISBN 0-07-707558-7

Library of Congress Cataloging-in-Publication Data

Clark, Frances A.
  Total career management: strategies for creating management
  careers / Frances A. Clark.
     p.   cm. – (The Henley management series)
  Includes bibliographical references and index.
  ISBN 0-07-707558-7
  1. Career development. 2. Personnel management. 3. Management –
  Vocational guidance. I. Title. II. Series.
  HF5549.5.C35C53   1991
  658.4'07124 – dc20   91-22728

1234CUP9432

Typeset by Cambridge Composing (UK) Limited
and printed and bound at the University Press, Cambridge

Contents

Preface

Why write a book for general managers about career management? They have made it, they know what it takes to be successful. They must be the best placed people to manage the careers of their own managers. This kind of thinking is still found today, but in my dealings with senior managers as a consultant, project manager, trainer and career development adviser, I have noticed that there has been a marked shift away from the certainties implied here about career and management.

What is the explanation for this? The present general or senior manager is likely to be the product of several organizational schemes or circumstances that explicitly or implicitly moved likely candidates upward and onward, assuming that success meant promotion and promotability could be predicted in the long term. Provided a person's career was correctly managed from above, individual and organizational requirements could be neatly dovetailed. This is no longer the situation. Career paths are less visible and those that are do not stay the same for very long. Many senior managers I meet have doubts about where they are heading and believe that their own careers can no longer provide a template for those of their own managers on whom they depend so heavily for their own career success. This feeling is heightened by the increasing devolution of human resources issues to the operational units and an expectation that general managers will have the prime responsibility for dealing with them.

Furthermore, competitive pressures, restructuring of whole sectors and delayering of organizatons, coupled with political, demographic, social, legal and technological changes have affected educational and employment expectations and practices. The result is that a multitude of options now exists for different patterns of working relationships between individuals and organizations. To be successful, the general manager needs committed and adaptable people but cannot be inflexible about their career needs in case they leave. Nor is being *laissez-faire* about careers possible because objectives must be achieved and organizational expectations met. The general manager is caught between the traditional prescriptive career demands of the board above and the new career flexibility requirements of the managers and their partners and families below. Furthermore, managing careers has costs if it is done well and costs if it is done poorly. On this basis alone it should merit the close attention of senior managers. How then can all these different needs be reconciled to the satisfaction of the individual and organization?

Awareness of all the diverse elements in this picture is surely the first step, followed by a rethinking of the general managers' role within it. Role images that are usually used for general managers, such as an artist mixing colours to get the right effect or shade, or a pattern-maker using existing shapes to make new ones, would suggest creativity and flexibility but also that general managers are manipulative or have focused on a vision of the ideal manager. Words such as 'coach' are often used but these assume a particular, desired, direction. Perhaps the future image is more that of partners building a jigsaw. The starting point is a random arrangement of variously coloured pieces (skills, abilities, motivations) within certain constraints (organizational, social and so on). Pieces may be chosen according to all kinds of different criteria: shape, size, colour, image and so on. The intention may be clear to the person picking them up, but not necessarily to an onlooker. The picture emerges slowly and is only obvious when the working career is completed. Whichever image is most helpful, creativity, flexibility and balance are key attributes in achieving the right combination in creating future careers for managers.

This book sets out the elements of career management (environmental issues, challenges, problems, organizational processes and policies, individual planning and strategies) general managers and their staff can work on together to create the new combinations and permutations of working life that we call 'career'. The terms 'general' and 'senior' managers are used interchangeably throughout the book because job boundaries between them may be difficult to draw. Moreover, job titles may mean different things in different organizations. For example, those who have a responsibility for business units may not be called *general* managers and, alternatively, there may be *senior* managers who are accountable for producing business benefits through managing a diverse range of specialisms. Furthermore, no special chapters are devoted to the impact of work on the family, and vice versa, or to women's careers. These two issues are so fundamental that they surface throughout the book.

General managers who need frameworks, guidelines and examples of best practice should find the book useful in tackling their own careers as well as those of others. After all, if they are uncertain where they are going, they are unlikely to offer the required support and encouragement to their staff. Younger managers, professionals and human resource specialists could also use the book to anticipate some of the dilemmas and choices with which they will be faced or on which they may be expected to advise so that they will be better placed to enlist the support of line managers in developing and executing career plans.

To encourage readers to apply the material to their own situations, a number of 'action questions' for senior managers, managers and human resource specialists have been added at the end of the chapter. They are posed in the form of questions rather than points to follow as that would be overly prescriptive. As the tenor of the book is the encouragement of flexibility, no one 'best way' is advocated.

Acknowledgements

First of all, I wish to thank the managers who have shared their experiences of their careers with me over the years. They remain anonymous but not unacknowledged.

My thanks are also due to the reviewers of the manuscript for their encouragement and constructive suggestions. I hope they are pleased with the result.

Finally, my family watched the project grow and take over domestic life. They bore the brunt of this with patience and cheerfulness, which is why this book is dedicated to them. In particular, my children, Nicola, Antony and Christopher, who have yet to embark on their careers.

1
Introduction

1.1 The meaning of career

Ask a group of managers what they understand by the term 'career' and a variety of interpretations and experiences will be offered, usually without consensus, although they may use the word freely. Talk to personnel managers and those involved in management development about careers in their organization and before too long the conversation will expand into many related areas of human resource management and business strategy, laced with a number of problems:

> We have a high-flyers group but there won't be enough openings for them, even assuming some will leave.

> A 35-year-old in the top cadre asked me what the organization is doing about her career.

> Executives we've been carefully grooming for several years are now refusing to move to where we need them.

> Competitors view our organization as a rich poaching ground. What good does career development do us?

> We're expanding very fast but lack suitable senior managers to be accountable for new product areas.

> The fast-stream scheme is demotivating other competent managers.

> It's difficult to generate any movement to allow middle managers to grow in competence and experience.

If these observations about careers sound familiar I would suggest that, in part, the fault lies with the lack of an accessible body of terms, assumptions and frameworks to which general or line managers can turn. They are the ones who have to make sense of career issues that may require decisions either as a senior manager or in a personal capacity. It is therefore worth pausing to see where the various notions of career have come from, what assumptions they make and what limitations they have. This review is not intended to produce the ultimate definition of career, but it will provide some ideas that will be elaborated on or complemented in later chapters

1

The very word 'career' carries with it implications of rivalry, positioning, speed, only one winner, ultimate and graded success, individual effort and acclaim. These ideas are still embedded in organizations, sometimes unproductively. They persist in current phraseology in 'fast track', 'flyer', 'staying the course' and in appraisal systems, promotion policies and remuneration.

Sequential careers

In the early 1970s, a career was still seen as an orderly progression of development over several years, achieved through holding down more responsible jobs through a series of promotions. By 1976 other, though not incompatible, ideas were being introduced.[1] A career could be any sequence of jobs that required personal commitment and development. While many non-career jobs could be carried out with high commitment but little development, a career needed both; moreover, careers were demanding, might even be unplanned and only became apparent with hindsight. At the same time, the idea arose that a career was as the individual perceived it over a lifetime: a sequence of work-related experiences and activities and their associated attitudes and behaviours.[2]

Internal and external careers

A distinction[3] was made between the internal (or subjective) career – that which has special meaning to the individual, encompassing needs, aspirations, specific goals and self-identity – and the external (or objective) career. The latter is what employing organizations, search consultants and others will see in the form of a chronology of job changes listed on a CV. The external career is itself conditioned by environmental factors and the organization's response, which will be covered in Chapter 2.

At this point the reader will sense the potential for discrepancies between an *organization's* notion of a career for the manager and the *manager's* own views (not necessarily comprehensive or totally coherent) about certain elements of career (advancement, commitment, personal development). The term 'career logics' has been used to describe the wider interpretation an observer tries to make of the manager's reasons for moving between jobs.[4]

Work histories

One study of UK managers[5] focused even more strongly on the idea that a career should be broadly defined as a work history, as, for many managers, prospects were thought to depend on luck and politics rather than on a personal career plan. Moreover, the work history was itself conditioned by the non-work situation, which could not be ignored in making interpretations. The authors found that career concerns took second place to the family, a factor to which organizations might have to pay increasingly more attention.

Transitions in careers

So far, mention has only been made of a single career, with the implications of some underlying continuity. That assumption does not hold true nowadays with individuals using Master of Business Administration (MBA) qualifications and other forms of training to achieve quite radical transitions. For example, a 33-year-old assistant secretary in a Civil Service department obtained an MBA and began a career in management consultancy. This Civil Servant had achieved a level of advancement in his first career that might be the pinnacle of another's life-long efforts.

Parallel careers

Allied to these sequential and transitional situations is the notion of a *parallel* career. This kind of career is illustrated by the manager in a hi-tech company who is also developing his wine exporting business; by the accountant who is heavily involved with his professional institute – a prelude to being employed by them; or by the management consultant directing a telecommunications business run by his wife and an associate.

Life and career stages

There is another major concept involved in interpreting careers. The idea of life stages interweaving with career stages has become of current concern in thinking about careers. People are said to devote the early part of their work experiences to exploration, which usually goes on until the ages of 30 or 35. This is then followed by a period of achievement and establishment until, between 38 and 45, the mid-career and/or mid-life 'crisis' appear, perhaps together. Children may have left home, the manager's career may have peaked and life and work values are re-assessed, often very hurriedly. This time of upheaval may give rise to the second career,[6] a much more frequent occurrence now as firms do not feel able to offer careers for life, for reasons to be explained later in Chapter 2.

Conclusion

To sum up so far, we can think of a career as a sequence of jobs or activities, planned or unplanned, involving elements of advancement (subjectively defined), commitment and personal development over a defined period of time. The significance of these jobs or activities (the internal or external career), their interpretation by others looking for a 'career logic' or consistency and the definition of time scales will provide considerable variation in interpretation. The second and parallel career phenomena, overlaid by the interaction of personal and work life increases the complexity. All this makes careers difficult to plan and predict in the ways individuals and organizations have done in the past. Nor can we assume that the 'life stages' of adulthood are similar for all. Indeed, the notion of an organization alone managing an individual's career is an impossibility if 'career' is viewed as having all or some of the elements mentioned above.

Career management in organizations will only become coherent if individuals are prepared to offer some (if not all) of their private thoughts and agendas within the work context and general managers are able to respond in a flexible way. The variety of terms and the managerial concerns cited earlier should therefore come as no surprise with the major changes that are occurring today in the world of work.

1.2 Models of career

Pictorial

It can be helpful to think of careers in pictorial terms, as demonstrated by Figure 1:1. In situation A, the triangle, everyone enters at the bottom of the organization, which is usually a small, entrepreneurial company, and works their way up by awaiting the 'tap on the shoulder' in response to their contribution. By contrast, the ladder, B, focuses attention on advancement through climbing up a recognized organizational hierarchy. The careerist can see which sequences of jobs to follow and can plan a preferred career path in a stable environment. Nowadays, problems are occurring with this model since its very existence is being questioned as the number of 'rungs' is being reduced because of organizational restructuring. One senior manager in a division of one of the utilities commented:

> I'm at the second rung from the top. But now all the rungs beneath me have been taken away and I will no longer be leading a team of engineers. At the same time, changes are occurring in reporting relations above me. I reckon I have 18 months before the ladder gives and I take charge of a new operation or leave.

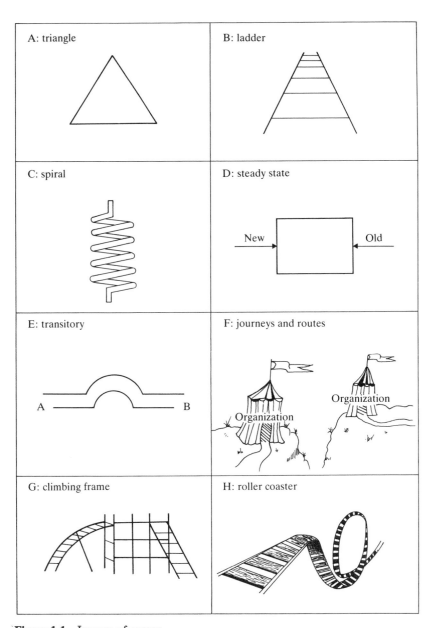

Figure 1.1 Images of career

The 38-year-old manager quoted above is ready for the spiral career (C in Figure 1.1) – an upward and outward move. A changing environment is forcing the manager to think about a radical career shift (into the new functional role of general manager) accompanied by increased seniority if the manager outperforms the competition for the job. This overcomes the limitations of the ladder model, which assumes that there is always some gradation in work content or skill between the rungs.

Alternatively, in both high- and low-growth industries (both of which can generate career uncertainties), the steady state career[7] of D can offer the manager with a specialism a niche to occupy or an area to expand. Management consultancy, computing, bio-technology – all can sometimes provide such a career pattern through the application of the same skill in different environments.

One example is a physics graduate. He had a doctorate in computer science and experience in a sales function with an IT vendor when he was taken on by a management consultancy to advise on state-of-the-art information technology. He quickly spotted a niche by developing managerial decision support systems, first in demonstration form, to interested directors and clients. This soon developed into consultancy assignments with blue chip clients for board-level information management support systems. Needless to say, a promotion followed within a year even though initially the area had been peripheral to the core business and organization values. However, once the area was expanding and he was recruiting additional staff, the star decided to leave to set up his own business. The three-year transitory career (E in Figure 1.1) as a management consultant (combining sales and technical skills) had refocused his longer-term career aspirations of working for himself and only choosing assignments that interested him. It had also acted as a bridge to enable him to achieve his ideal type of work.

The remaining career concepts shown in Figure 1.1 are relatively recent and reflect the greater uncertainties generated by rapid sectoral and organizational change. One view of managerial careers[8] is as 'stories about journeys and routes through and between organizations' located at different points on a varied landscape (F). Some of the 'paths and stories are well-trodden and well-known, others are improvized and haphazard' and some just 'peter out'.

In this scenario, careers can begin in a vague way. For example, in a start-up operation, senior managers may be asked to write their own job descriptions, set their own goals and acquire external resources. On the other hand, careers may actually disappear as the demand for a particular technology, service or product declines, leaving a once key person in the middle of nowhere.

The climbing frame[9] of G in Figure 1.1 is another way to deal with managerial careers. Here, organizations have variously shaped frames, with differently spaced rungs, both vertically and horizontally. People may take hold of the frame at different levels and can move across, down or up the frame (organization) in different ways and in different sequences. This structure allows for more flexibility of individual choice while recognizing the internal constraints organizations face when moving individuals to develop their careers.

For good measure, an anecdotal model is added: the roller coaster (H in Figure 1.1). There has recently been much activity in some sectors, in particular those of the financial and professional services. Acquisitions, mergers and divestments consume managerial effort and internal company resources and lower the core business activity. Overlaid are the personal feelings of uncertainty and stress. Since the roller coaster is going so fast, the route is not always clear to the traveller, the depressions may appear unexpectedly and need to be managed before the hills can be climbed. Not only may the riders not know where they are going, but things may happen so fast that they are unsure just where they've been. One senior manager told me of a transfer from one foreign-owned commercial bank to another. By the time the manager arrived at the new employer's premises, four out of the five board members who had been responsible for the recruitment had moved on, *en masse*, to a third employer. The manager felt that the support and power base of the position had disappeared, leaving the manager exposed far too early in a career. Meanwhile, the difficult situation the manager had encountered at the first employer (the integration of a newly acquired stockbroker) had been swept away by the announcement that the two were intending to part company (interestingly, the acquired broking operation had had four owners in the past seven years – uncertainty about careers there must have been justifiably very high).

These views of careers are important as they offer seven alternatives to the traditional ladder concept when considering manager's careers in organizations. It is common to hear forecasters say that the ladder will disappear. It may well be correct not to expect it to stretch from the bottom to the top of organizations, but it could still exist within and between various functions and start at different levels within organizations. The point here is that we can no longer believe that this view of careers is the only or the desirable one. To deal effectively with career issues, general managers will need to reassess the importance that their organizations attach to offering careers and help individuals to assess the opportunities.

1.3 The importance of career development

Career development for individuals is a vital prerequisite for organizational development. To prepare for change, organizations need committed people and one way to ensure that this happens is to have developed managers not only implement change, but handle its consequences well for their own and others' benefit.

Recent and future trends.

The fact that changing circumstances are forcing senior managers to take a more active, enabling (rather than directing) role in the careers of their staff in order to meet their own objectives and those of the organization is a marked shift away from the recent past. The last 15 years have seen an alteration of emphasis in how careers should be managed. There has been a move away from the traditional 'the organization knows what is available (and what is best for you)' approach and centred instead on the corporate philosophy of 'everyone is responsible for his or her career – don't expect us to plan it'. A key reason for this was that in the UK during the late 1970s and early 1980s, rapid changes, unemployment and recession forced organizations to 'let go' of careers and encouraged a 'survival of the fittest' attitude. Indeed, the previous sections on the meaning and models of career reinforce this idea of the difficulties of trying to create a master plan, both from an individual point of view and for organizations.

In the 1990s, change and uncertainty will be even more pronounced, fuelled by the continued restructuring of whole industrial and commercial sectors, new organizational forms, altered societal values, and a demographic (not just specialist) shortage of skilled labour (see Chapter 2 for more details about this factor). Can organizations now afford the *laissez-faire* policy on careers to meet the challenges of the 1990s? It would appear not, judging by the efforts being made to provide opportunities to attract and retain potential managerial recruits, such as expenses-paid recruitment fairs for potential 'euromanager' attendees, sponsorship of MBAs, study leave and overseas projects, to name but a few – all geared to enhancing individual careers.

Frames of reference

This book aims to pursue a more balanced path between the prescriptive and *laissez-faire* approaches by viewing the 'enabling' of careers as the legitimate province of the organization and of senior managers, while not removing final responsibility from the individual staff member. The general manager, by virtue of the title and broad responsibility, needs to have a wide perspective on the issues raised so far when considering careers.

In this context, it is worth noting that there is variation in the way organizations and writers use the terms 'career planning', 'career management' and 'career development'. One convention has been to reserve 'career planning' for activities assumed to be carried out by the individual (for example, goal setting, self-awareness, decision making). 'Career management' is what is practised by the organization (counselling, job rotation, controlling promotion, announcing vacancies, appraisal and so on). The outcome of these two activities is said to be 'career development'. It is obvious that these distinctions can become blurred. For example, organizations run development centres to help individuals become self-aware and engage in goal and life planning exercises. On the other hand, some individuals find it impossible to plan at all. Other individuals actively engage in management of their careers by seeking opportunities in the organization or contacting search consultants. The outcome of these activities may not be career development within the organization and in some cases may be geared to a holding operation rather than to personal development. The broad convention is followed here but the reader is asked to accept that this cannot be rigidly applied.

1.4 Perspectives on careers: environmental, organizational and individual

Career management (the term is used in the modern sense of enabling) as an area of managerial competence is fundamental if the organization is to meet its strategic objectives and if the individual is to derive a sense of purpose, motivation and self-esteem. Meeting these two classes of needs has costs (financial and in terms of opportunities, goodwill and energy) if career management does not occur to the satisfaction of both parties. In particular, absenteeism, turnover, performance decrement and atrophy of skills are some of the consequences of failure in this area. There are also costs if career management *does* take place, as it will involve a substantial investment of money, time and energy in the human assets of the organization. Therefore, general managers cannot afford to avoid the issue, having, as they do, responsibility for the 'bottom line'. Satisfied people are usually committed, productive and receptive, willing to work hard to achieve the goals of the organization. An interest in helping to manage the careers of others is therefore not an optional extra. At the very least it can be one important yardstick, for managers to measure their own success by how much they encourage the success of others. Some

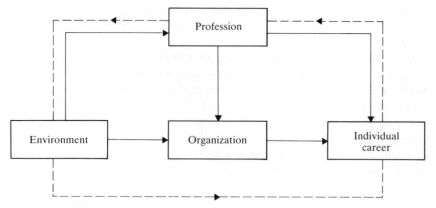

Figure 1.2 Managing career development

organizations recognize this by insisting that before managerial promotions can be implemented, a manager has prepared one or more successors. These successors will only be found if they feel the next move will enhance their own careers, so their managers have to take an interest in them to ensure that their needs are met.

The framework

As a process, career development is unlikely to be satisfactory if considered only from one perspective and without looking for interactions between the influencing factors. A broad tripartite framework for considering careers is recommended (see Figure 1.2): the environmental, organizational and individual elements. These not only affect careers directly but are linked to each other.

Also shown for the sake of completeness but not a central part of the context is the term 'profession'. Professional bodies are not just those of the established professionals, such as accountants, lawyers and engineers, but other specialisms, such as computing and marketing. Many professional bodies have a substantial influence on careers via the environment, the organization and the individual by virtue of their status and position in society, their publicly stated values, licensing practices, body of knowledge, tools, techniques, training and experience requirements. Moreover, some are laying down specific guidelines for continuing professional education. General managers need to be aware of and to analyse these complex interactions, anticipate their consequences for individuals and integrate them into their organizations by taking them into account in their management of their human resources.

The elaboration of this three-fold structure provides the sequence of subsequent chapters in the book. General managers are first asked to consider the environmental factors and the corporate response to them in Chapter 2 before taking up the organizational challenges of facilitating managers' careers in Chapter 3 and dealing with their staffs' career problems in Chapter 4. To be successful they will also be required to work within the various career-linked organizational processes that affect careers observed in Chapter 5 (recruitment, mentoring, appraisal, internal networks). They also have the ability to influence organizational policies about high-flyers, late recruitment, converting specialists into line managers, promotability, child and family care and counselling – subjects covered in Chapter 6 – that enable or constrain careers. The need for responsiveness and flexibility to the environmental and organizational factors (see Chapters 2 to 6) means that senior managers will also require a sensitivity to individual career needs. The processes operating within individual career planning and development (passing through life stages, choosing, motivating oneself and discerning patterns in one's career) are covered in Chapter 7. Moreover, this awareness can be supplemented by at least a general knowledge of self-help techniques, both as an aid to staff development and the general manager's own career. In the light of self-analysis, individuals may need to formulate their own career strategies (see Chapter 8) and be helped by their general manager in executing them.

1.5 Conclusion

The framework provided by Figure 1.2 for examining careers therefore serves not only as an analytical tool, but as a structure for the book as a whole. It should act as a constant reminder of the elements that the general manager has to juggle and reposition when facilitating and managing the 'career jigsaw' of other managers and his or her own. The creation of managerial careers therefore involves a constant seeking out of new opportunities for enhancing personal development and the structures and relationships to support them.

Action questions

SENIOR MANAGERS

What have you done recently to further your own career?
Which images of career in Figure 1.1 best fit your organization?
Are there different images for different functions?

Do you feel able to offer assistance and support for your staff in their own careers?

MANAGERS

How responsible do you feel for your own career?
Is it clear what help and support you can expect for developing it and from whom?

HUMAN RESOURCE SPECIALISTS

What do senior managers and their staff understand by the term 'career' in your organization?
Do you distinguish between career planning, career management and career development? Where does the effort in your organization lie?

References

1. Rapoport, R., and R. Rapoport, *Dual Career Families Re-examined*, Martin Robertson, 1976.
2. Hall, D. T., *Careers in Organizations*, Goodyear, 1976.
3. Schein, E. H., *Career Dynamics*, Addison Wesley, 1978.
4. Gunz, H., 'The Dual Meaning of Managerial Careers', *Journal of Management Studies*, Vol. 26, No. 3, May 1989.
5. Nicholson, N., and A. West, *Managerial Job Change: Men and women in transition*, Cambridge University Press, 1988.
6. Levinson, H., 'A Second Career: The Possible Dream', *Harvard Business Review*, Vol. 61, May/June 1983.
7. Driver, M., 'Career Concepts and Career Management in Organizations', In C. L. Cooper (ed.) *Behavioural Problems in Organizations*, Prentice-Hall, 1979.
8. Nicholson, N., and A. West, op. cit.
9. Gunz, H., op. cit.

2
Environmental career drivers and the corporate response

2.1 Introduction

Macro changes in the external environment of many organizations are causing them to refocus their perceived roles and strategies. These various external changes, as well as having a direct effect on organizations, have also had an impact on each other. They reinforce a climate of continuing change and raise questions about what actions organizations need to take to survive and develop. These changes also have implications for the management of human resources and are affecting employers' and employees' attitudes and perceptions about careers.

Factors affecting career opportunities

Figure 2.1 sets out seven of these major factors. The headings are necessarily broad, containing within them many facets. Only a few links have been made in the diagram to keep it simple, and provide a context for career management.

Starting with political changes and working clockwise round the diagram, the combined interactions of these various factors can be seen. The agreed removal of trade barriers to create the single European market of 1992 has also intensified commercial pressures for acquisitions and joint ventures, requiring organizations to rethink the type of manager that will be required and the career and other incentives that need to be offered. Commercial pressures have, in turn, resulted in a search for new organization structures, that are leaner, decentralized, responsive and flexible. These changes have led to a questioning of traditional employment policies, whether they are necessarily applicable to all. 'A career for life'

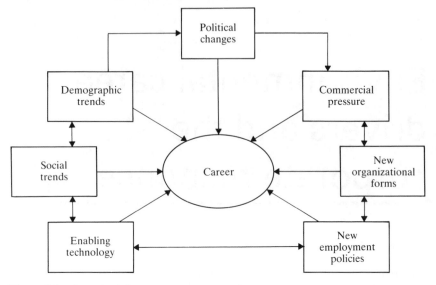

Figure 2.1   A context for career management

has come to be seen as neither the only or the desired option, for organizations and managers alike. Furthermore, new organization structures and employment policies are, in part, dependent on enabling technology, which has led to a re-examination of the nature of managerial work, global IT systems and telecommuting. Enabling technology has itself influenced expectations about the relationship between the extent and legitimacy of career demands and the quality of life: robots can do dirty or dangerous work and cellular radio and related technology can make the executive accessible 24 hours a day, by land, sea and air. Social aspirations and desired lifestyles have had their influence on demographic trends. Smaller or no families, increased divorce rates, single parenthood and ageing populations are all part of the social fabric.

The scheme proposed can be used as a check-list against which the general manager can consider career issues. This chapter will expand on each factor in turn. Some have individually received much attention from the media and it is not the purpose of this chapter to present an in-depth appraisal of each. However, consideration of their impact on career development has remained fragmented and is therefore worth highlighting. The second part of the chapter will outline what some organizations are doing in response to the impact of these macro changes on careers.

2.2 Demographic trends

Much has already been written about the demographic trends for the 1990s but it is perhaps useful to restate some of the known (and perhaps not so well-known) facts so that the implications for career management can be discussed.

The shrinking pool of young workers

There will be a decrease of some 25 per cent of 16 to 19-year-olds in the work-force by the end of the 1990s to a minimum of 2.6 million, after which the numbers look to increase to approximately the same level as the early 1990s. Total student numbers in higher education are set to follow a similar pattern, picking up again after reaching a low of 113 000 in 1998. Already, nearly 90 per cent of those qualified to enter higher education do so, making attempts to increase qualified manpower from this source difficult. Other European countries are likely to have similar problems and the generally predicted differences in the shortfall for the year 2000 are marked for the 15 to 19-year-old group:

- West Germany 42 per cent
- Italy   32 per cent
- Britain   19 per cent
- France   10 per cent.

Spain, Portugal and Japan are in a slightly better position than Britain. In Japan, for example, the reduction will be only 7 per cent. Ireland, in contrast, will have no problems.

The figures for West Germany, however, relate to the period before unification, so their shortage could be relieved in the short term by the influx of immigrants of German origin from parts of Eastern Europe.

An increasing number of older workers

To offset the one million decrease in the under 25s within the UK, there will be an *increase* of approximately one million 25 to 34-year-olds (and an ageing population in general, which will increase social security costs and the level of employers' national insurance contributions). Therefore, career development and 'fast-stream' schemes relying on the entry of the under 25s to feed them will need rethinking. Moreover, the 34-year-olds at the top of the band are those who will be nearing the run up to the so-called 'mid-career crisis' and special attention will be needed from their employing organizations.

Married women as a source of workers

The greatest untapped source of employees is married women – some estimates exceed over a million. A recent report by the Institute of Manpower Studies[1] suggests that two major factors (not unrelated) are responsible: the traditional caring role, which can often preclude full-time work, and discrimination. The report goes on to say that removing these barriers would mean more women would be employed in higher status jobs. The career management implications of this are far-reaching, requiring flexibility and sensitivity to the family situation and demands that have been noticeably missing in recent years.

Skills shortages are increasing

Skills shortages will become more severe, especially among professional, scientific and technical staff, exacerbated by poaching from countries in the European market whose community graduates are nearer 26 or 27 when they start work.

Many large companies that are household names were failing to achieve their desired graduate intake just before the recession of 1990/91 set in. However, these particular skills shortages could be alleviated if there were to be a substantial influx of well-qualified immigrants.

More specifically, skills shortages are predicted in IT, financial work, mechanical engineering and chemistry and in specific employment sectors, such as construction, the civil and public service sectors and the utilities.

Organizations' responses

The organizational response to this situation has been found to be lacking, as indicated by a number of surveys. The National Economic Development Office[2] (NEDO) survey of 2000 firms showed that most employers were over-optimistic about their ability to compete for young recruits and three-quarters of them were focusing their efforts on competing better for young people. Half of the employers reported problems in recruiting them. Moreover, few had looked to alternative labour sources and even fewer had considered options like job sharing, career breaks, new contractual arrangements, childcare schemes or flexible retirement policies.

The NEDO report also examined strategies developed by more innovative firms. These were to retain and retrain their existing work-force and tap alternative labour (women and older workers). They were buying time to rethink their traditional approach to recruitment, training and retention and adopt the right mix of actions in relation to business needs. Planning and integration of solutions with existing human resource policy was seen as a critical success factor and multisite organizations opted for local rather than central solutions. All this points to a need for general managers to become involved in developing a suitable infrastructure for creating managerial careers within their organizations.

Personnel Management[3] surveyed 1000 personnel professionals to identify what their companies' recruitment practices were in response to the demographic downturn. In an analysis of responses to 'newer improved employment conditions' in the last two years, the top three were:

- higher pay, 66 per cent
- performance-related pay, 36 per cent
- company cars, 28 per cent.

Other changes introduced to improve recruitment included:

- training for new recruits, 54 per cent
- retraining existing staff, 48 per cent
- widened selection criteria, 41 per cent.

Career development was not even considered. The prevailing view of the article was that recruitment was the 'key to fulfilment of corporate plans'. General managers, it seems, would be wise not to put all their eggs into the recruitment basket.

Atkinson[4] classifies the responses organizations are making to the situation as:

- *on the chin*: work overtime, lower selection criteria
- *compete*: improve image, liaise with schools, raise pay
- *substitute*: recruit and retain women, older workers and reduce wastage
- *create*: improve skills of work-force, improve deployment.

Firms' responses, he maintains, tend to start with an on the chin attitude and, as the situation becomes more difficult, they progress from tactical to strategic ones. Most businesses are said to be currently in an on the chin frame of mind but will be forced to compete until high costs drive them to substitute other sources of workers for the dwindling pool of traditional recruits.

They will then move to the creative response, which forces them to make the best use of the work-force they have and ensure that they are less vulnerable to interference from competitors. The demands for creativity in developing managerial careers will be greatest here. They will rely on an imaginative use by their general manager of company policies and resources that will be combined in a unique way to obtain specific, local effects. To illustrate this last approach, some fairly radical responses are

Table 2.1   Recent examples of radical responses to the skills shortage

Organization	Response
British Telecom	Retraining telephone operators as engineers. Opening technical apprenticeships to 40-year-olds.
British Airways	Recruiting female sixth-formers and students to train as pilots.
Hewlett Packard	Training to turn selected arts graduates into electronics engineers.
Ford	Encouraging female entrants to apprentice training.
Civil Service	Raising the graduate entry age from 37 to 52.
Police	Recruitment age raised from 30 to 45.
Armed Services	Recruiting older people who can live at home.
IBM	Offering MBA courses to operatives in a manufacturing plant.

set out in Table 2.1. They have been collated here as examples of what can be achieved.

The responses listed in the Table clearly require major policy shifts to enhance the motivation, development and deployment of existing as well as new staff.

2.3 Political changes

This section will focus on the effects of the single European market of 1992 on human resources management and, in particular, careers. It will consider briefly the need for 'euromanagers', recruitment and training requirements and employment legislation, all of which impact on careers.

Euromanagers

The group management development manager of a large UK-based multinational engineering and construction company with a turnover of over £3000 million raised the question of whether a euromanager was what the company needed. The board's policy was one of devolution of responsibility for products and services at national and local level. Therefore, there was little point in trying to effect secondments of people at middle or senior middle management level unless there was a very specific requirement, for example developing a new business operation. Where a secondment did occur, once a 'local' had been recruited and trained, the visiting manager would depart. The company were therefore adopting a 'wait and see' policy in relation to the need for euromanagers.

A completely contrary viewpoint is that the euromanager is vital where companies (marketing products using a fairly uniform approach worldwide) need multiculturally sensitive individuals who are not blinkered by work exposure in only one national culture. Some companies, such as Philips Electronics and Ford (Europe), have already made a strategic commitment by placing their central R&D functions in Europe. Other multinational organizations have also concentrated their efforts for the development of different products in one location: DEC has moved its worldwide telecommunications headquarters to France.

Some commercial sectors have a head start as they are, by their very nature, internationally focused, such as international banking, dealing in securities and consultancy. In such cases, the orientation of the euromanager is, by definition, compulsory.

A stance that reconciles these two opposing positions is that there are certain functional areas (determined by strategic needs) where it is clearly cost-effective to take a global approach (R&D, product development), while for others, such as marketing and sales, national culture exercises a strong influence on preferences. However, any organization that commonly uses a task force approach in encouraging new initiatives is going to need euromanagers. The question is, in what quantities?

RECRUITING AND TRAINING EUROMANAGERS

If the organization wants some euromanagers, how can they be recruited and trained? Europeanization goes far beyond mere fluency in a language. Understanding of cultural values, the economic infrastructure and business practices are key elements. Some firms, such as Hoechst, are sponsoring exchange schemes for young recruits and managers in Germany and the UK. The course lasts two years and participants can obtain a diploma from the relevant chamber of industry and commerce. The emphasis is on young staff acquiring experience before their mobility is restricted. At the very highest level, companies are endeavouring to have task forces and boards composed of different nationalities to develop a European perspective and to exploit the strengths of national characteristics.

If individuals in the UK wish to develop into euromanagers, there are already European companies who are willing to help them by recruiting in the UK, such as Siemens, Elf and Thomson. In addition, the graduate shortage mentioned under 2.2, Demographic trends, could be affected by European poachers. Degree courses abroad are four to six years in duration and some students resit examinations. The age range on graduation is therefore higher (graduates being 24 to 26 years old) than in the UK and there are those who have to serve two years' national service as well, making a new Continental recruit from 26 to 28 years old, whereas British graduates are generally between 21 and 22 years of age.

So, age for age, the Continental recruiters in the UK would be obtaining qualified professionals with management experience. The expectation is that, with the harmonization of professional and other qualifications, the outflow will be greater from the UK than the inflow because of attractive standards of living and pay on the Continent. The harmonization of professional qualifications is critical if employees are to understand and accept the qualifications of professionals from other EC countries who wish to work here (or vice versa) on the same terms as those from the host country.

LEGISLATION

Potential legislation affecting employment is an area for general managers to note. The Community Charter of The Fundamental Social Rights of Workers – or the Social Charter as it is more commonly known – is the key means for implementing the Commissions' strategy on social rights, which relate primarily to employment. This is of particular significance as the commercial activity increases in anticipation of the single European market.

A fear is that increasing competition, acquisitions, restructuring and relocation could lead to an unwelcome situation. Firms could establish operations in member states with the poorest social conditions and least stringent standards of employment. It is thought that this could then cause a downward drift in standards from those of the more advanced countries. Opponents (for example the UK) see the Social Charter as a possible threat to a deregularized labour market, which would be likely to increase their labour costs.

A key issue in all this is the free movement of workers within the EC. In particular, there are proposals to provide for:

– worker participation in public limited liability companies
– maximum working time limits
– minimum standards of health and safety
– disclosure of information to employees, in particular on major changes and the consequent consultation
– atypical contracts, for example for part-time and temporary work
– minimum wages.

Initial reactions in the UK have, at best, been indifferent and in some cases hostile. In view of the current interest in the UK in customer service, flexibility, quality and people-oriented organizations, these reactions are difficult to reconcile.

THE EFFECTS OF EMPLOYING EUROMANAGERS

What then are the implications for the general manager and for the careers of those who are managed? Assuming that many British organizations will be recruiting euromanagers or working with them in task forces, allowances will need to be made for their different needs as they are likely to be older, married, more mature but less managerially experienced. Professional qualifications will be broader-based than those of their British counterparts and they will expect to enter the organization at a relatively high level, requiring a tailored induction programme.

For UK nationals, the attractions of foreign companies will need to be offset by planned experience abroad (with suitable briefing and preparation) within their organization. Furthermore, general managers will need to be familiar with EC employment legislation when they or their subordinates are managing abroad to better understand the expectations of those coming from abroad to work in this country.

2.4 Commercial pressures and globalization

Commercial pressures are expected to intensify globally and this will be accompanied by an increase in restructuring. Sir John Harvey Jones has warned that 50 per cent of Europe's factories could close as one of the measures to combat overcapacity. The trend is towards very large European companies and the UK makes a rich picking ground, as the takeovers of Morgan Grenfell by Deutsche Bank and of Rowntree by Nestlé have shown. The rationale for the increase in acquisition activity may be defensive, serving as a bulwark against non-European competition – acquire or be acquired.

Take-overs

British firms are more liable to take-over for a number of reasons. In particular, they tend to hold a short-term view of performance whereas the Continentals will look at success over, say, a ten-year period. Another is the relative amount of detail of accounting, financial and shareholder information that is available to prospective buyers. A third cause is the restriction on the permitted size of a company enforced by the Monopolies Commission.

While the UK is an easy target for European firms, British firms find it difficult to acquire European operations as they are not so open. Some, like the former West Germany, have a large number of family-owned concerns. Frequent defensive tactics in Europe are finding national consortia to fend off bids, government intervention and required compliance with legislative and other restrictions. So far, the world economy has espoused the principles of competitive trade (the battle for the customer) and adversarial trade (total market dominance). However, a new principle of reciprocity[5] is now thought to be emerging as countries bargain for similar access rights to each other's markets. In Europe, the removal of tariff barriers is an illustration of such an attempt to counteract the fragmentation of 12 separate markets. However, this still leaves it vulnerable to inroads by the Japanese and American competition.

The effects of globalization

While immediate concerns may be with Europe, the globalization of business is adding complexity to a fast-changing world. Some sectors (such as financial services) are already geared to this uncertainty in terms of attitude, internal managerial practice and client service. Other sectors have yet to appreciate that the expectations and interplay of main world financial centres have to be understood when making decisions.

Because of enabling technology, reactions can be so fast that markets can be adversely affected. Indeed, one view is that the macro-economic system has become so complex that it can hardly be described.[6] Therefore expectations that it can be analysed and predictions derived from it are bound to fail. Attempts at control must necessarily be focused on specific problems.

Globalization of business is also having structural effects on different internal functions. For example, Merrill Lynch recently opened a data-processing centre in London's dockland. Now over 100 dataprocessing staff have been made redundant as the bulk of processing will be carried out at head office in the USA.

The changes that have occurred and what these have meant

Within the UK, general environmental turbulence has resulted from:

- *deregulation*: airlines, telecommunications and financial services
- *major restructuring*: within business sectors and organizations – mergers, acquisitions, divestments, decentralization and pruning of staff numbers
- *environmental lobbying*: water purity, nuclear and chemical waste.

More specifically, organizations are now leaner, more competitive and flexible in their activities, having had to cope with the new business changes that have occurred in virtually every sector:

- *private sector*: the setting up of joint ventures, such as Honda and Rover, and also restricted-life companies, for example, Rosehaugh-Stanhope
- *financial services sector*: for example, organizations ignoring 'traditional' business boundaries, such as building societies offering insurance and banking facilities, banks offering mortgages, insurance companies linking with estate agents, retail banks acquiring and divesting themselves of merchant banks and brokerage operations
- *utilities*: for example, through privatization, passing from a break-even philosophy to a profit orientation to satisfy shareholders, some acquiring or being acquired by foreign operators, meeting regulatory controls covering pricing and standards of service and maintaining better customer information systems for improved marketing
- *public sector*: the Civil Service acquiring a more commercial orientation and adopting a policy of agency status and the health and education sectors adopting a budgeting/cost centre approach to managing their operations
- *local authorities*: tending to subcontract work to outside agencies, assuming more of a broker's role in, say, providing finance for children's homes and supporting projects while retaining an inspection and quality control function.

Cost cutting

Underlying all this is a tendency to drive costs down through contraction and decentralization in order to compete internationally. Job losses have occurred right across the board, although middle management have been a particular target for savings. The recent cuts at BP, for example, have been particularly swingeing, and at the highest levels. The cost-cutting trend is not restricted to firms in trouble. Cadbury Schweppes, Plessey, IBM and Ford, to name but a few, have carried out similar proactive exercises.

One way to reduce costs and encourage growth is demonstrated by British Airways Speedwing Technologies, a holding company for business developed from its information management function. It sells IT products and services on the open market. BA declined to hive off the whole of its information management department as IT is so fundamental to its competitive capability and some core functions need to be retained to serve the business. These examples of widespread restructuring have enabled new organizational forms and employment policies to be considered, which will be discussed under 2.5, New organizational forms, and 2.6, New employment policies, respectively.

To summarize

The commercial pressures, fuelled by international competition and the single European Market, could generate much uncertainty about organizational career paths. With the prevalence of UK companies being acquired by European ones (rather than the other way around) and the effect that new corporate and international cultural styles can have on organizations, these doubts could become more marked. There will be pressure on general managers to keep abreast of the global and European scene, understanding in some detail how the EC works, and lobbying, if necessary, on business matters. In particular, they will need to be aware of what niches exist and what skills are valued, both for their own careers and for those of their subordinates.

Within the UK itself, there will be a requirement to manage new businesses or multiple businesses within their organizations, operate with foreign partners and trade confidently in new markets. In the light of this, managers (who by this time may be out of date with their original specialism) will have to reassess the worth of their own and their teams' experience when called upon to meet these new challenges.

Because of the restructuring and contraction that has become a way of life in organizations, general managers will need to anticipate possible changes far enough in advance to prepare their team for alternative careers, possibly within a new form of organization.

2.5 New organizational forms

The existence of a fast-changing environment requires responsiveness and flexibility. Atkinson[7] has argued that firms will need to achieve flexibility in at least three areas relating to employees, which contrasts with notions of the traditional hierarchical bureaucracy. These areas are:

- functional
- numerical
- financial.

An explanation of these areas is given in the following paragraphs.

Functional flexibility

Functional flexibility would facilitate the quick redeployment of staff to meet the firm's requirements. At a craft level, this means a blurring of old divisions, such as those between mechanical and electrical engineers. In other cases, it requires a complete change (say, turning redundant women telephone operators into British Telecom engineers).

In one small (160 people), fast-growing computer business software company I visited, there was no organization chart, because small groupings formed and re-formed with ease in response to customer demands. The firm's structure evolved around the needs of the customer, with 70 per cent of the employees in customer-related functions such as marketing, sales, telemarketing and customer services (technical support, bespoke programming and engineering). The average age of the staff was 26 years and within 5 years they could expect to be managers. They were thus very receptive to the idea of functional flexibility as a means of career development since they had all prospered under it.

Numerical flexibility

Numerical flexibility enables the head count to be easily adjusted for short-term changes through a more individualized contractual relationship between managers and staff. The engineering, construction and IT sectors are good examples of this arrangement. However, one large engineering company ran *so* 'mean and lean' that it found itself without a pool of staff from which to select its cadre of future directors and senior managers and had to start actively recruiting again at the required levels.

Financial flexibility

Financial flexibility as a third option allows, among other things, an organization's remuneration system to be sensitive to the differences in and supply of various skills and professions and to reflect the state of the market. The organization is not hampered by a fixed grading system or other form of differential between employees. In one multinational company, IT staff were difficult to recruit and almost impossible to retain for long. The company used short-term remedies such as market supplements and over-promotion. This led to grade drift and dissatisfaction among employees in other functions.

These numerical and financial flexibility policies apply to contract staff who are always paid more than permanent staff. However, they lose traditional benefits (for example, holiday and pension rights), security and the potential of a career.

Functional, numerical and financial flexibility operating together

Atkinson has projected a possible organization structure (see Figure 2.2) that enables these three types of flexibility to co-exist.

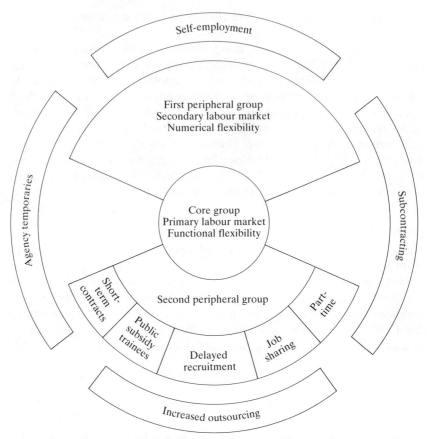

Figure 2.2 The flexible firm: projected organizational structure
Source: Reproduced, with permission, from Atkinson, J., 'The Changing Corporation' in D. Clutterbuck (ed.), *New Patterns of Work*, Gower Publishing Company Limited, Aldershot, 1985.

THE FULL-TIME CORE GROUP

A full-time core group (for example, managers, designers, technical professionals) would carry out firm, specific activities. Security would be given in exchange for functional flexibility. This implies for example, cross-functional working in multidisciplinary teams in the short term and, in the longer term, being willing to keep training and retraining as the situation demands, learning new skills.

For this group, there would be a commitment by the organization to provide suitable careers and rewards as it would be less able to recruit replacements with the critical organization-specific knowledge.

THE FIRST PERIPHERAL GROUP

This group would also be full-time but the jobs would not be firm-specific and replacements from the external labour market would be easier to find than for the core.

The jobs would have no prospects and little training and development would be carried out. Turnover would typically be higher than for core jobs, enabling numerical flexibility to be achieved. An example of this is the retail and hotel and catering sectors where such a situation exists among employees in the lower grades.

THE SECOND PERIPHERAL GROUP

This group would offer both functional and numerical flexibility, depending on the nature of the employment contract.

The jobs would not be firm-specific and would often be part-time or could be put on hold by delaying recruitment. Again, there would be no long-term future and the minimum necessary training would be given.

EXTERNAL EMPLOYEES

The last group would be external to the organization in the form of agency temporaries, such as word processing staff, staff from executive leasing agencies, self-employed people, such as consultants, subcontractors (small firms), outsourcing, that is, any other help who would not receive any training and whose contracts could be terminated at short notice. An illustration of this is British Petroleum.

The company recently decided to contract out most of its computer services as part of a cost-cutting initiative to save around £100 million. Again, there is no notion of 'career' for these people as far as the organization is concerned.

Problems with this structure

Problems reported by managers whose organizations are partially implementing such a structure are:

- difficulty in deciding which functions or areas should be staffed in which way
- deciding which management style should apply to which group
- generating commitment among staff.

What is clear is that with the widespread practice of decentralization, the use of profit and cost centres and the flattening of organizational hierarchies, more experimentation is occurring in how and where people are employed. What is not so clear is just what the organization's level of commitment is to such employees (and vice versa) and what effects this may have in the future if practices grow piecemeal rather than as part of a longer-term strategy.

The shamrock organization

Charles Handy[8] proposes this organization as an alternative to the traditional bureaucracy.

THE CORE GROUP

Similarly to Atkinson's model, there would be a 'core' consisting of professionals, managers and technicians who would constitute the collective knowledge of the organization – for example, professional partnerships, consultancies, advertising – and project the corporate image.

Here promotion would be fast and the upper echelons would be reached quickly by committed, future-oriented staff. They would have invested heavily in terms of time and effort in reaching the top and results would determine their remuneration and therefore their lifestyle.

THE CONTRACTUAL FRINGE

This would be the second group (corresponding to Atkinson's external group of both individuals and organizations) whose payment would be for results and in fees rather than for time and wages. Management's task here would be to specify closely what results were expected, to what standards and by what date. The methods would be left to the contractor.

Managing this relationship would require commitment by both parties. Poor work would signal the end for any future contracts. Equally, payment of minimal fees and extracting every right would put the organization at the end of the contractors' list with a note 'undertake only if desperate'.

THE HIRED HELPS

This third group would be people whom organizations would employ as and when the need arose.

Comparison of the flexible firm and the shamrock organization

While the two models only make provision for career development and training for the core, it can be argued that this could be short-sighted, both in terms of quality and in long-standing relationships. Exit and entry to the same organization may not be a once only event as it now tends to be.

A freelance consultant was employed by one of the largest UK-based consultancies for his skill in distribution and logistics as a consultant. He then left to become freelance and then rejoined the organization as a director. As this example demonstrates, it is therefore worthwhile for general managers to keep in touch with leavers as well as (selectively) training them for any skills if the name, quality and reputation of the firm is at stake. Similarly, a more caring attitude may be needed for the hired help category whose contact with customers or telephone manner can make or break the image of the organization. Alternatively, as the labour market tightens for the young, these groups may be a pool of untapped talent.

Other options

Parallel to the developments of the flexible firm there are a number of operational arrangements between large and small companies that have the potential for career development for the managers of both parties.

LINKED-SUBCONTRACTING

Linked-subcontracting, such as that found in the construction industry where there is a trend to offer managed contracts, provides the small firm with, say, the chance of fitting out an entire leisure centre complex. Managers in the smaller firm grow and expand their horizons by being part of a project that would have been beyond their scope and reputation had they tendered alone. Some individuals may join the larger company to bring specialist knowledge in house to help develop business. Specialist managers from the larger company may transfer to the smaller company in a general management capacity to broaden their managerial capability, knowing that there will be supportive relationships with their 'new' client.

PURCHASER–SUPPLIER RELATIONSHIPS

Close purchaser–supplier relationships, such as those adopted by Marks and Spencer to improve quality, can provide career development opportunities through mutual staff training and secondments.

One manager in an electronics multinational had specific responsibility for wholesale distribution of products for the lighting sector. He joined a large electrical wholesaler as a managing director, thus enabling and improving relationships between the two companies.

A similar transfer occurred in an investment bank when there were no prospects of internal promotion and salary increases. A manager of financial products transferred his skills and knowledge of portfolio management to a current client with a treasury department.

SECONDING STAFF TO OTHER COMPANIES

A third possibility is when large companies seek opportunities for innovation, especially in the IT vendor or software sectors. They may second a manager to help develop a product or service, with the smaller company providing most of the capital and other resources. That way, the large company can minimize the risk and the smaller company gains by obtaining an added boost to a development that it wanted to take forward anyway.

A variant of the previous situation is when the two organizations have a mutual need to develop complementary parts of a product. If the product is hi-tech, the small firm may provide leading edge software or equipment, applying its expertise in a way that it could not otherwise have done if overcontrolled by the procedures of a larger firm.

The enabling company

Lessem[9] points to another form of organization – the enabling company (see Figure 2.3). It exhibits various functions that evolve with the needs of the organization.

THE FUNCTIONS

Manager and staff are the core organization, supported by external consultants for training, PR, software and financial advice. These provide an independent service, as a group of self-employed individuals who are networkers. F-International is an example of such a networked service.

External entrepreneurs are brought into the orbit of the organization as *intra*preneurs. Such a situation occurred when a management development operation employed part-time the director of a small company to redesign and deliver courses in project management.

Third, craftsmen (including professionals) provide specific skills for a particular job by being subcontracted when needed.

Finally, the innovator can be brought into the organization through joint ventures where risks are then shared. For example, a large

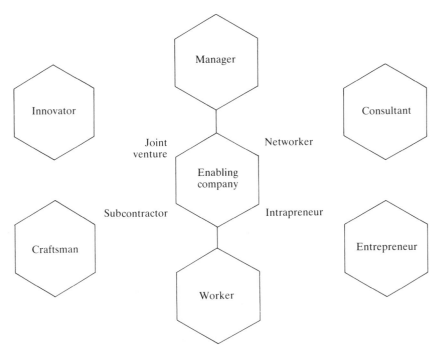

Figure 2.3   The enabling company: functions
Source: Reproduced, with permission, from Lessem, R., 'The Enabling Company', in D. Clutterbuck (ed.), *New Patterns of Work*, Gower Publishing Company Limited, London, 1985.

accountancy-based consultancy developed a telecommunications capability through joint project work with a small innovative firm.

THE STRUCTURE

The outline structure of such a company is kept simple. A chairman acts as a strategist and arbiter for a managing director and a development director. The managing director markets existing products and services and develops business opportunities, employing the subcontractors. The development director coordinates the joint ventures, networking and entrepreneurial activities, which are not easily accommodated in the more formal structure.

EFFECTS ON CAREERS

The implications for careers inside and outside such an organization are the need for individuals to maintain a wide and competent group of contacts, able to market their own services and respond in flexible ways to business opportunities. Careers then take on a fluid and chameleon-like form.

Corporate olympics

Moss Kanter[10] sees the future organization as competing in the 'corporate olympics' and combining power with agility. She suggests that the three strategies to achieve this are:

- organizational restructuring to find synergy
- the use of partnerships or alliances to get work done
- identifying 'new streams', or, new possibilites, within the organization.

THE EFFECTS ON CAREER

The implications of frequent restructuring for careers (with the loss of hierarchy and central staff) are clear. Hierarchy will lose its importance and force as a controlling factor of careers.

The increased need for lateral cooperation and communication across functions or business divisions will concentrate career influences at the peer level. This is because judgements of competence and opportunities to develop new businesses will tend to occur at this level in the future. The partnerships or alliances (with the increased permeability of organizational boundaries and increased sharing of information) will allow for working relationships that could create movement back and forth between organizations.

Finally, the new streams (the creation of new ventures from within, regardless of function) will provide many opportunities but will also be accompanied by proportionate risks. Within each project there is, therefore, the occasion for enhanced career development (success breeds success) and expansion, or career demise (one is only as good as one's last project).

MANAGING IN SUCH AN ORGANIZATION

With all these potential organizational variants it is obvious that the choice of organization, not only in terms of sector, image, financial health and culture but also of structure, will have an impact on managers' careers and the direction they are able to take. If these new forms of organization are to work then senior managers will have to find suitable employment policies for them.

2.6 New employment policies

It is not the intention here to give a complete review of all forms of employment policy. Rather, there is a need for the highlighting of certain ones that impact on careers, some of which have achieved more visibility in recent years or are new in concept. Although they have grown in application in a piecemeal fashion they apply to managerial as well as other staff and do provide the general manager with a range of options to respond to the new forms of organization mentioned in the previous section. The forms of flexibility within the employment pool are:

- self-employment
- part-time working
- fixed-term contracts
- job sharing
- flexitime
- variable shift working
- annual hours
- V-time
- career break schemes
- sabbaticals.

Self-employment, part-time working and fixed-term contracts

Self-employment is increasing (by over 50 per cent in the last 10 years) and some 33 per cent of the British work-force are not full-time employees working in a single job. Nearly 25 per cent of the UK work-force are working in part-time employment, mainly through choice; and the UK is one of the EC countries with the highest proportion of part-timers.

The holding of multiple jobs is also increasing. It is possible to be in full-time employment and, at the same time, work freelance in the evenings and at weekends. Equally, some types of work, such as operating telephones, can be combined with other jobs, such as security work, just as a freelance may hold several substantial fixed-term contracts, each running to a particular term with different organizations and, in some cases, renewable.

Career development here is the responsibility of the individual and the freelance may have to take every opportunity for learning when working for different organizations. Talking to staff, examining what techniques are being used and using databases and libraries where permitted are some obvious ways.

Job sharing

Job sharing for professional and other staff has been in operation for some time in clearing banks, parts of the Civil Service, the computer industry, training and educational establishments and in local government. The takers for these positions are varied: single parents, those supporting the elderly, potential retirees and mature students wishing to gain additional qualifications. The scheme can be operated in ways to suit the particular needs of the organization and the individual. This can mean:

- working alternate days, weeks, six-month periods
- dividing the day, week or parts of the year.

The advantage of this for careers is that it is a permanent part-time arrangement and likely to attract at least the minimum training. There is also some commitment on the part of the employer as well as job visibility. Both of these are helpful if the individual wants a full-time job later on.

Flexitime

Flexible working hours (FWH) takes a variety of forms. In flexitour, employees choose their starting and finishing times and work the same number of daily hours. A second variant allows them to alter their starting and finishing times each day. A third option permits them to vary their daily hours around a core time. A fourth arrangement called maxiflex enables daily hours to be altered as desired without the need to be available for a core period. This requires the concentration of effort in a longer working day.

Flexible working hours has the benefit of attracting a wider pool of labour. Single parents, those with difficult journeys and specific, personal needs benefit as FWH enables them to accumulate and carry forward time. For the organization, it helps to motivate staff because they feel more in control of their lives and this can help to ease recruitment, retention and unexpected absenteeism for visits to solicitors, banks and so on.

Problems may occur over the definition of various terms. Core time, accounting periods, maximum accumulated time that can be carried forward and other issues (such as to which grades or functions it applies) are points that need careful thought. Some areas, such as production in a continuous process workflow, can limit the flexibility possible, but personnel, administration and other support services are more amenable to this arrangement.

If internal agreements can be reached, flexitime can provide a useful and cost-effective way of coping with rush jobs, year-end accounting peaks and waiting time between projects, to name but a few instances.

In the Civil Service, one assistant secretary wanted to change her statutory working hours from the current 10am to 6pm to 8am to 4pm, with a core time of 9am to 3pm, but found her deputy wanted the same. This would have left the department without senior cover for two hours. The consequence would have been unacceptable for the provision of external legal services (such as when a response was needed to parliamentary questions), so a compromise of these hours for alternate weeks was agreed. Both parties were then able to benefit from the arrangement.

While FWH is useful, a pattern that is too idiosyncratic might reduce the indirect contact and visibility at work with those who choose more conventional hours. This could affect membership of the informal networks that are so important to the development of careers.

Variable shift working

Shift working patterns, once confined to manual or operative workers, can now be found in technical and professional jobs, such as computer or hi-tech support services. They also occur in some parts of the financial services sector because of the globalization of business and the settlement requirements for certain transactions.

At Philips in Belgium, the idea of shift working at the weekends in one factory was unpopular until the factory concerned paid the same for a 24-hour shift at the weekend as a 38-hour shift over 5 weekdays, thus recognizing the compensation needed for unsocial hours. The workers then alternated their shifts to provide a felt-fair pattern of working.

Graduates may not always appreciate these situations when deciding on a career within functional areas such as production. Therefore general managers who operate shift systems within their units need to ensure that those who work them know what is involved at the start and see that their contact with others does not suffer unduly.

Annual hours

Another opportunity for variation is the use of annual hours or the flexible working year. Employees contract with the organization to work a fixed number of hours per year and are free to choose their own working times. After three to six months, employees can renegotiate an increase or decrease in hours. An example of this way of working is Kaufhausbeck, a retail store in Munich. The scheme was introduced after careful analysis of both the numbers of customers dealt with on various working days and the preference for hours of work among staff.

This arrangement helps overcome seasonal or cyclical fluctuations in workloads and enables a closer matching of hours of business with customer requirements. Other reported gains are greater productivity (because working chosen hours is more motivating and leads to less absenteeism), a flexible work-force and the ability to tap into part-time labour.

From the employees' viewpoint, it offers choice and the ability to change hours according to need (with suitable agreed notice) and allows the security of a regular monthly salary. Pilkington Optronics and Volkswagen are two other organizations known to be using such schemes.

There are clearly some jobs that require specific hours of attendance in addition to satisfactorily performing various tasks and employers need to look closely at what will suit their needs best in selected parts of their organizations. Careerwise, this could provide individuals with opportunities for self-development outside work.

V-time

V-time provides an option for full-time staff to reduce their working hours for an agreed period with a corresponding reduction in salary. Benefits are reduced on a pro rata basis and there is a guaranteed return to the previous job. The time may be taken in the form of shorter days, weeks or in blocks (such as around the school holidays). The Alliance and Leicester Building Society have introduced a pilot scheme permitting time off in school holidays for those with children.

It is also useful for responding to health problems of the employees or their dependants. V-time can also be used for gaining new skills or qualifications to enhance a career. For example, an MBA programme may require residential weeks and attendance for examinations that the employer would not normally consider granting.

Career break schemes

Career break schemes are increasing in popularity. While open to men *and* women, they are more often taken up by women as they provide a 'safety net' in the form of an extension of time after the 29 weeks' maternity leave. This is an important consideration as fewer than 7 per cent of women in the UK return to full-time work after maternity leave, although some 90 per cent return after a longer absence. NatWest Bank has been running such a scheme for several years and it is mentioned in their graduate recruitment literature. Barclays Bank and ICL also offer such a facility.

It helps to avoid having to make a choice between family *or* career as participants can return to work with no loss of job security. A break may be taken of up to five years continuous time or in blocks of shorter duration. During this time seminars, training and relief work are offered and any other relevant information to keep the potential returners in touch with the business. This ensures that self-confidence and expertise are maintained while reducing the stress of combining a very young family with career commitments.

From the organization's viewpoint, it ensures a return on the previous investment in education and training and provides a pool of trained people to cover for general sickness, absenteeism, holidays and peak business periods. Last, but not least, participants provide a model, particularly for women, of how to combine family and career demands successfully.

Sabbaticals

Sabbaticals are also being considered as a way of rewarding service to an organization. In Australia, 15 years with the same employer earns a sabbatical. In Sweden, the practice is accepted in a variety of occupations and in the UK the John Lewis Partnership provide such a scheme for employees (this area will be covered in more depth in Chapter 4).

The benefits of these policies

These 10 employment options provide general managers with a means of accommodating their own and others' needs as their personal and career needs change. However, they do need careful appraisal and monitoring if business requirements are also to be met.

2.7 Enabling technology

One reason for organizations taking new, decentralized forms and considering alternative patterns of working as part of their employment policy, is the existence of communications and information technology.

Information systems

Integrated text and data processing systems (used by insurance companies) and transaction clearing systems (used by banks, building societies, for airline reservations and so on), while removing large numbers of clerical staff in organizations, have also allowed a decentralization of many routine processes. They have enabled improved speed and quality of customer service, which in turn are fundamental to maintaining a competitive edge.

On-line enquiry systems (such as BT's maintenance and repair system) offer improved service and productivity through managerial ability to monitor, control and switch resources quickly within certain constraints.

Moreover, information from these types of systems is accessible from a number of locations. For example, salesmen can anticipate the availability and delivery of items from stock, another factor enabling decentralization without loss of control, while making careers more local.

With less need to perform routine checks on methods and results (since much of this process can be built into the system through error checks and summary reports), layers of middle management roles have been removed. This achieves faster internal communication and, at the same time, exposes jobs that are not adding value. Therefore, there is a certain impetus to improve or develop existing managerial jobs that can create other career opportunities. For example, the head of computing of a small building society found that once on-line distribution systems had been introduced to branch offices for serving customer transactions, his role began to focus less on the technical aspects of IT and more towards customer care in product delivery.

Expert systems

Electronic mail and management information systems, which allow managers to access information from a corporate database, have become more widespread. These, coupled with systems for professional problem solving (for example, modelling real-life situations to generate options for action), make the managers' role and style far more proactive than in the past. Additional information for comparative and evaluative purposes, thus extending and enhancing managerial abilities, can also be accessed from professional and public databases. Furthermore, the general manager has a far greater ability to carry out spot checks on what is occurring within the organization than ever before. Using IT, managers can diagnose faults remotely (such as monitoring problems in reservoirs or reading meters), reducing the old difficulties of multisite management. The transformation of dealing rooms into walls of computer screens in investment houses bears witness to this need for ever more information. Expert systems and the design of special executive operation rooms to equip executives with better facilities for decision making are also gaining greater acceptance in many industries (for example in oil exploration and pharmaceuticals respectively).

Expert systems allow room for a second opinion and enable greater delegation of authority and responsibility in decision making. For computer-literate managers, IT allows them to tackle new tasks and acquire new skills to enhance their careers.

Information technology for manufacturing and engineering

This has transformed the capacity to create new products (for example, through computer-assisted design), manufacture them, in some cases in an entirely automated factory, and link all this into the distribution and logistics systems.

With IT, flexibility of production has been created through complex scheduling of orders and materials instead of being geared to immediate utilization and scale of production criteria. Dangerous, dirty and repetitive work has been reduced for operatives. Also, a less crisis-orientated production environment has left time for the exercise of higher level decision making skills from management regarding the business and future plans. Traditional boundaries between jobs have thus been broken down (as between purchasing, materials management and production) and old career paths no longer exist.

Career implications of the new technology

The implications of all these developments are clear. General managers need an up-to-date understanding of information technology to approve its purchase and maintenance and to oversee its management to:

- obtain a competitive edge in the delivery of products and services, while adding value to jobs, particularly at the managerial level
- control and master the formal information flows within the organization (as well as the informal ones) and to be proactive in their use
- ensure that the maximum benefit is extracted in product design, manufacture and delivery.

Unless this is done, many careers are put at risk through the possibility of business objectives not being met. Moreover, boundary changes (brought about by IT) between jobs, functions and countries mean that there is a greater flexibility in the direction that careers are able to take. For example, the use of IT as a marketing tool and product delivery mechanism enabled one manager to become the European marketing director responsible for interactive video techniques in selling personal computers. While some may thrive on this kind of challenge, the blurring of boundaries and loss of specific and well-tried career routes can be disturbing for others and need to be watched by senior managers.

Remote, or, teleworkers

Another vital aspect of information technology is how the working routines of the office have been changed and the extent to which certain types of employee need to be on site at all. Remote, or, teleworking (staff communicating with their employers by computer, telephone and fax) has been growing over recent years, although not to the extent that pundits have been predicting. In recognition of the growing interest and the need for such arrangements, British Telecom has produced its own 'guide to working from home'. There is, however, a complication in that the official statistics on which such forecasts have been made do not differentiate sufficiently to give precise analyses of exactly who are teleworkers and who are self-employed. In fact, those who use technology to work from home can be: 'corporate itinerants' (say, insurance salesmen), 'freelances' (authors, architects, accountants, systems analysts) or 'traditional home-workers', running a small craft business. These cut across the official statistical categories, making comparisons difficult because of the variety of occupations covered and the blurring of the distinctions between those who are truly employed and those who are self-employed.

However, remote working provides another option that the senior manager might need to consider in facilitating the careers of others in the more flexible organization of the future. Indeed, property developers are even building work homes to cater for this situation.

THE BENEFITS

From the organizations' viewpoint, remote working allows a reduction in headcount and costly overheads without losing the skills and abilities of staff. Employees are generally paid for the job (rather than on a time used basis) thereby, it is claimed, increasing productivity. Well-publicized experiments specifically in teleworking have been those of Rank Xerox, ICL and the software house F-International. However, other organizations and sectors have long been used to a remote working basis: insurance companies and their agents, some management consultancies use associates working from a home base, planning inspectors in the department of the environment and financial advisors. All these can provide models for others to follow. At least three main issues need consideration where such options are used:

1. management and control of such workers
2. contractual arrangements
3. training and career implications

otherwise the advantage to all can be reduced.

MANAGING REMOTE WORKERS

While the benefits cited for remote workers are autonomy, flexibility, control over the type and pace of work and lack of the need to travel every day to a fixed workplace, these very characteristics make it more difficult for managers to supervise them in the traditional way. Objectives, results, standards of performance, time scales and contingency plans need to be more carefully specified. In some cases, the manager has a reduced or no formal authority over the remote worker.

There is little opportunity for the 'fine tuning' that can be achieved through casual contact in the office to overcome unforeseen problems and give encouragement and moral support. Special efforts, therefore, need to be made to ensure that quality control is maintained and training may have to be given where necessary.

Last but not least, efforts have to be made to reduce feelings of isolation and increase corporate identity – even if the worker has also contracted to work for other organizations. This can be done through product seminars, conferences or newsletters, to name but a few methods.

CONTRACTS

Contractual arrangements must be particular to the firm concerned and the nature of the work done. Corporate itinerants (such as sales and insurance representatives) are usually paid by salary and commission and freelances by fees. ICL's home working division gives employment contracts to its workers rather than using them merely as freelances to develop software. They have holiday and sick leave and a retainer of 16 hours per month. ICL also provide workers with the equipment they need.

CAREER STRUCTURES

For those remote workers who are direct employees of an organization, there are usually well-defined career structures. Even so, there is still a fear that the lack of visibility of the home-based could prejudice career opportunities. For the self-employed or freelances, employability means being up to date and developing themselves. Recognition by peers and the client base is the way their careers develop. For the self-employed associates of Allied Dunbar, selling financial services, training is tied to selling products. The right to sell more complex or high-return products requires a licence, thus ensuring that the necessary training is not avoided by associates.

As an option for employment, remote working can be a very attractive situation. For senior managers it can offer a way of substantially reducing overheads. For those at particular stages of their career or with special or temporary family circumstances it can provide the freedom they need. It also fits with some of the social trends relating to autonomy of lifestyles and personal values.

2.8 Social trends

The social trends to be considered here are only those that have an impact on careers. They have been grouped under:

– expectations
– values
– problems.

Expectations

Livelihood and career are necessarily intertwined. A career brings with it a style of life and a need to sustain it. Material standards of living have increased generally and it took substantially less time in 1988 for a man with a non-working wife to earn basic goods and services than it did in 1971. Now, at least, two thirds of all homes are owned by their occupiers and are in better condition, providing a ready focus for the spending of earnings.

In one part of the country, the managing director of a manufacturing organization questioned the long-term motivation and commitment of a young work-force whose average age was 26. In the short term, they were prepared to adopt whatever working hours the company wanted so that they could buy and furnish their own homes to a high standard. Once these needs had been met, there was a fear that there would be no incentive to be loyal and remain adaptable for the firm concerned. There was no thought about developing themselves, let alone a career and it was believed that this could lead to long-term instability within the firm.

With the satisfaction of such expectations comes a change in the minimum acceptable standard of living. There are now an increasing number of dual career couples, some of them 'dinky' (dual income no kids yet). Together they achieve a lifestyle at middle management level that would normally have only been possible for very senior management within their organizations. Their own career mobility may be severely restricted if they cannot see equivalent opportunities elsewhere for their partners.

Another group targetted by sales organizations are the 'woopies' (well off older people), owning major assets such as their own home and possibly those left to them by their parents. These may be seeking early retirement to use their assets and pensions to enjoy themselves or start another business or career at around 50 years old. Thus their internal careers are what motivate them and they will not be easily assimilated into organizational plans unless they are allowed the freedom to pursue their own agendas.

Values

Two separate but related societal values are the questioning of authority and the values behind the rise of the knowledge worker. Some 20 years ago, the author heard the head of a branch of the Civil Service say at a lecture that he wanted to commission a study on how to 'make people accept authority'. Several in the audience wondered why the problem had not been posed as 'how can we encourage staff to participate in a responsible way'. The person concerned had not realized that senior managers cannot merely *dictate* what must be done – persuasion, nego-tiation and partnership are the values in the workplace for setting objectives, carrying out plans and monitoring performance. Power does not reside merely in a job title or position. Expert knowledge, access to rewards (however defined) or to information and participation in networks are just some of the more widely recognized sources of power in organiz-ations. They can be used by both managers and their staff. People now expect to be consulted and have control over their work. That expectation applies also to their careers and its impact on their life outside work.

'Small is beautiful' and entrepreneurship are values strongly related to the restructuring of organizations and new organizational forms. They also serve as alternatives for the rejection of the authoritarian values of the bureaucratic organization. Smallness is seen as offering flexibility, auton-omy, control, variety and creativity. In fact these are all attributes long recognized by empirical researchers as providing job satisfaction and the prevention of the negative effects of stress.

Second, the value placed on knowledge and skill as the wealth-producing resources is seen in the rise of 'knowledge workers' – those who, through the application of their professional skills, add value to the work of their organization. In parallel with this is the decline of manual, dirty or dangerous jobs, now increasingly being done by machines.

Learning and professional values control opportunities for entry into a livelihood and career and being up to date is a prerequisite for maintaining that livelihood. Obsolescence, even for a short time, could mean unemployability. Learning how to learn is an essential skill for survival. Professional and self-development are therefore two ways in which general managers can motivate and reward their managerial staff and facilitate their careers. At the same time, being accountable for highly trained and employable staff can only be beneficial to the development of general managers themselves.

Taken together, the values considered here point to trends in how managers expect to be managed and, by implication, the way their careers can be developed. Personal attention to individuals' expectations and values in relation to training and to organizational and occupational career opportunities will be the norm required.

Problems

Social trends also indicate an increase in particular problems. Consider the following facts from the latest published figures from the Office of Population Censuses and Surveys:

- nearly 40 per cent of marriages end in divorce
- single parents now raise 14 per cent of all children
- the heaviest drinkers are separated and divorced men, their average weekly consumption being 26 units per week compared with the 'safe' level of 21 units
- some 25 per cent of all households are single person (compared with 12.5 per cent in 1961), which is not merely an increase in the number of elderly – the greatest increase in numbers living alone is in men under 65 years old, with the potential for loneliness and isolation increasing.

It would be very surprising if some of these social trends did not affect performance and interpersonal relationships with colleagues in the workplace.

THE IMPACT OF PROBLEMS ON WORK

In a recent study on the impact of divorce on work,[11] the impact both on day-to-day work, such as attendance, hours worked, overtime, achievement, observed performance, and on long-term work and career, such as aspirations, satisfaction, motivation and career values, was noted.

In the first main area – impact on day-to-day work – more women than men improved and more men became worse. A similar pattern was noted for the long-term and career aspects. Overall, 41 per cent said that working relationships had changed into friendships, with care and support being offered, especially with peers.

The study highlights two main points. First, women seem to adjust better to the effects of divorce by investing their new energies in their career. The authors speculate that this is not an alternative for men because that energy investment has already been made, hence their adjustment is not so good. Second, the organization is an important source of social support as colleagues can lend a sympathetic ear.

The study is also illustrative of the wider impact (often not formally recognized) of personal and family life on work. That work will intrude in and disrupt family life has in recent years been widely tolerated, but the reverse has not been true. Personal problems are, as far as possible, kept out of the workplace. Managers have traditionally been wary of recognizing them for fear of having to cope with something outside their normal repertoire of skills. If appraisal causes them anxiety, counselling is seen as carrying even more unknowns and risks. Nevertheless, the expectations, values and problems that staff bring, directly or indirectly, to the workplace cannot easily be ignored by senior managers. They are likely to intrude on work performance or career decisions and, as such, will demand attention.

Conclusion

In conclusion to the first half of this chapter, Table 2.2 provides a summary of the main impacts the various environmental drivers (or determinants) have on careers. It is not intended to be comprehensive, but it illustrates the complexities facing general managers in the management of their own and others' careers. While complexity may be hard to manage, it does offer a variety of options available to both senior managers and their staff in the definition and management of careers. Perhaps learning how to choose will become as important as learning how to learn in creating and sustaining managerial careers.

2.9 The corporate response and the influence of the board

It is obvious from the preceding sections that the sheer volume, diversity and complexity of some of the factors present in the external environment preclude any detailed prescriptive advice on what to do about careers and

Table 2.2   Environmental career drivers: a summary of their impact on careers

Demographic trends	Political changes	Commercial pressures	New organizational forms	New employment policies	Enabling technology	Social trends
Sensitivity to needs of ageing work-force. Rethinking of fast-stream schemes. Consideration of untapped sources of talent. Professional and scientific skills shortages. Efforts to ease sectoral shortages. Creativity in devising suitable company policies and use of resources to combat shortages. Training and re-training of staff needed.	Demand for the euromanager. Growth of European exchange schemes within multinationals. Increases in trans-national recruitment leads to increased opportunities. Awareness of employment legislation necessary for career management. Sensitivity to multicultural work teams (inducting, management, etc.) necessary for organizational performance.	Mergers and acquisitions lead to uncertainty of career paths. Anticipation of organizational impact of restructuring on people and their careers. Continual reassessment of worth of managers' skills and experience to manage new multiple or international businesses.	Decentralized, smaller organizations, earlier general management experience. Flexible organization has small core of flexible people. Career development and training mainly for core. Core security high – but transferability questionable because of organization-specific skills. Autonomous careers outside core. Greater variety of remuneration and benefits	Increased range of work pattern (e.g., FT, PT) and hours give flexibility to employer and opportunities for personal and career development for staff over larger term. Career break schemes and sabbaticals enable major development for career over short term (e.g., gaining qualifications).	Allows decentralization without loss of control, making careers more local. Remote working provides a spur to rethink how staff can be managed and what sort of career is wanted. Layers of middle management removed results in fewer career opportunities and exposure of non-value adding jobs. Less emphasis on routine checking of methods and results; more attention (potentially) to	Expectations about family and lifestyle constrain the demands that can be made of managers by the organization. Certain values such as the questioning of authority, small is beautiful and entrepreneurship determine what kind of companies managers wish to work for and what careers they choose to follow. The rise of the knowledge worker puts pressure on both general

schemes to consider when managing careers.

Closer alliances between firms opens up new career opportunities: secondments, task forces, transfers, etc.

Joint venture organizations/ enabling companies allow innovation in career paths.

Entry/exit to organization not once and for all events.

Importance of peer contacts and relations in career progression.

developing jobs and people. Databases and tools enable managers to be proactive and enhance and develop their potential.

IT enables staff at the customer interface to deal more directly with customers. Their careers are therefore more exposed to complaints of lack of service, etc.

Information technology in the manufacturing and retail functions has blurred boundaries between traditional jobs and old career paths no longer exist.

managers and staff to update knowledge and skills to prevent obsolescence and inflexibility and to provide a base for innovation.

Problems of divorce, single parenthood, loneliness, and use of palliatives are impacting on the workplace and career management will have to take these into account.

their facilitation within organizations. Rather, they provide a backcloth of areas that need to be checked out by individuals and employers alike.

One approach,[12] for example, focuses on the need to analyse several areas:

- *the whole person*: this is because societal values change and influence the meaning and centrality of work and the impact of family concerns
- *the different needs and interactions of various functional and occupational groupings and their career options and paths*: managers can then be aware of these differences as it will be they who have to coordinate their contribution to organizational effectiveness
- *the scope within organizational development for career development*: this will facilitate long-term change and make it stick by creating a receptive, critical mass already used to learning and teamwork
- *the culture and organizational history*: this will condition corporate history and values.

Other areas that could be researched internally are the attitudes to various types of employment policies, career initiatives, use of career services and counselling and so on. Indeed, some organizations already do this to make sure that their corporate response is adequate to meet the changes.

For research to be conducted and its findings acted upon, visible support from the board has to be given, otherwise managers will not accord it any priority. For some boards this will be difficult to accept if they cannot see its strategic significance. They may also feel careers are something merely personal or accidental or that staff should be able to see the next step themselves. All this is made more difficult if there is no human resources director on the board to argue the case.

Another way in which they can support initiatives is by approving objectives for the career management and development within their organizations. One construction company found that it did not have a suitable cadre of managers in place for its proposed business expansion. It therefore approved the aims of a senior management development programme, the criteria for selection onto it and the proposed changes to be observed in the managers after two years. The managing director then allocated three days to chairing a selection panel and discussing the results, opened the programme, attended course dinners to obtain instant feedback and devoted a day to assessing presentations of syndicate projects on corporate issues. Such visible commitment communicated the importance of the programme to the future of the company to other directors and to internal speakers. Over a two-year period, two members of the cadre were withdrawn as the result of promotion to director level.

Finally, the board has a vital role in communicating to general managers any business opportunities that might be vehicles for the development of key staff. That way, business needs are met and managers have a chance to become visible, which will, in turn, generate further career development.

2.10 Business strategy and human resource planning

Whatever alternatives for business strategy organizations select or tactics they employ to gain a competitive edge, the words 'quality' and 'people' soon appear.

Human resource planning

In the service industries in particular, where products, their availability, technologies, prices or fees are similar, quality of service is paramount and is only as good as today's people. Planning for human resources is therefore a key element for corporate strategy to be successful. It involves ensuring that the organization has the correct number of people with the skills it needs in the required location at the right time. It has to make informed guesstimates of the skills required and where and when they will be found. In doing this, a variety of methods may be used:

– extrapolating from past trends and the current situation to ascertain age structures and career paths
– using simulation models to make predictions about flows of staff given certain policies
– asking 'what if' questions to examine the impact of changes in business requirements or policies.

There must also be suitable action plans to cater for staff acquisition and development as well as for dealing with unforeseen contingencies.

In a major clearing bank in the UK, the head of the career development unit has joined the corporate planning team so that, for the first time, the characteristics of the employees and their needs can be more fully recognized. It will curb the natural tendency to want to simplify the complexity and unpredictability of people by reducing them to numbers, overheads, jobs and grades. This will also counteract the desire to 'feed' them into a manpower planning supply and demand model or system merely to forecast likely surpluses and shortfalls.

While these data are a necessary starting point for analysing and controlling the people resource, the term 'human resource planning' goes further to encompass their acquisition, management, development, motivation and retention. In fact, the ability to execute the planning is closely bound up with organizational processes and policies that will affect careers, and which will be considered in Chapters 5 and 6.

With the focus firmly on organizational careers, one approach[13] identifies four main functions of human resource planning:

– staffing – for those in current jobs and potentially in future jobs
– growth and development of individuals
– levelling off and disengagement
– replacement and staffing.

Business strategies

The way in which these requirements can be met depends on the type of business portfolio planning prevalent in the company or the strategic business units. Requirements for companies with a close group of core businesses will differ from the diversified ones in the required human resource strategy to service them.

THE BOSTON CONSULTING GROUP'S CLASSIFICATION

This well-known classification system of products and services, developed by the Boston Consulting Group, provides one approach.[14] The policy for human resources management of 'star' businesses (those with a high market share in a high growth rate market) is likely to be geared towards the consequences of managing ever-larger units and acquiring sufficient managers with entrepreneurial skills.

The 'cash cow' businesses (those with a high market share in a low growth rate market) will probably be big stable units requiring order, consistency and harmony of its managers. Caution will be required to conserve the gains, and profitability will come from good resource usage and tight performance management of people.

Where businesses have dropped into the 'dog' mode (those with a low market share in a low growth rate market), they may be running at a loss and need short-term, cost-conscious management. This style involves paring down resources, including people, and using stringent controls.

Finally, the 'question mark' businesses (those with a low market share in a high growth rate market) consume much capital investment and attention from management because of the uncertainties. Flexibility of employees is the key here and management will try to avoid the constraints of corporate policies.

The career implications for each type could perhaps be as follows:

- the stars will need to have individuals who relish being stretched through increasing responsibility
- the cash cows will not want too much staff mobility, but this could create a stale managerial culture
- the dogs might become a focus for two types: the tough company doctors or the plateaued manager who has ceased development
- the question marks might attract the go-ahead sort who expect to be highly rewarded if they can turn their businesses into stars.

However, the relative ease with which all this organizational planning can be done depends, among other things, on two factors, which are themselves related to business strategy: organization structure and growth.

Organization structure and growth

A helpful synthesis of the effects of these two variables[15] utilizes two key concepts: recursive and nonrecursive organizations combined with patterned and unpatterned growth. Recursive organization structures are ones in which each unit contains within it similar-looking sub-units. Examples could be stores in a retail organization, branches of banks or areas in major utilities. Each clearing bank, for instance, will have a branch manager and, above him or her, an area and regional manager. Thus, in recursive organizations there will be a higher proportion of similar managerial posts than will be found in a nonrecursive structure (for example engineering and chemical companies). This means that when vacancies occur there will be a naturally occuring pool of managers to fill them without the need for learning substantially new skills. The less recursive the structure, the more likely there will be a sideways move by an individual to or from a different kind of job.

Patterned and unpatterned growth also affect the internal labour market. A retail organization can expand by opening stores and may have a template of procedures to achieve this, drawing on a pool of internal experienced staff and developing their existing skills. However, they will be doing more of the same although there will be unfamiliar tasks and crises to handle. The career in such an organization will generally follow a pattern of a succession of moves with an expansion of scope, responsibilities and staff.

Unpatterened growth would occur when an organization sought to diversify into a new market or product area. For example, BAT has acquired insurance companies to add to its multiple interests. This kind of growth may mean that there is no precedent within the existing skills base for filling the vacancies and will therefore require a new approach. With this situation, the career paths may involve radical changes and appear to be disjointed.

The effects on human resource planning

It follows from the above that human resource planning is likely to be more complex in organizations that are nonrecursive and involved in unpatterned growth. Conversely, in those with a recursive structure and where expansion follows a pattern (or at least has some elements of continuity within it), the planning process should be easier. These considerations also constrain the usefulness of monitoring career movements merely in terms of people flows between grades and jobs and within job clusters and calculating their associated probabilities. This approach would ignore aspects such as personal motivation and organizational commitment. They will also dictate whether it is possible or desirable to have a centralized system for human resource planning.

All this does not negate the value of human resource planning but it does highlight the difficulty in expecting a template to suit all types of organization and produce generally applicable supply and demand models for situations that are becoming difficult to simulate. Merely copying best practice without analysing *why* it is so is also unproductive.

2.11 Succession planning

Succession planning is a much more specific process within human resource planning. It is a way of ensuring continuity of the organization's mission through its staff – in particular its senior executive cadre – by identifying internal replacements for existing posts and possible holders of future ones. Succession planning, given that the business needs have been identified, involves the detailed matching of information about positions and people.

Organizations will vary in the degree to which succession planning is carried out in their organizations. For some, it is only done for the next cadre below board level. Any extra resources can be drawn from a pool of high-flyers and from external organizations. For others, the process extends much further down. The problem with the latter option is that planned career moves become more difficult to implement smoothly as the number of people to move in the chain grows and is further complicated by open advertisement for some jobs and also external recruitment.

Succession planning depends, in part, on accurate and detailed information about the positions to be filled (level, function, location, skills and special operating conditions) and the people (function, skills, experience, performance, potential and so on) for its effectiveness. It also requires a sensitivity on the part of top management to the need for diversity to discourage clones.

Apart from the comprehensive profiling of what the post requires, the names of suitable candidates have to be found. They need to be drawn from as wide a range of sources as possible to prevent politics, nepotism and the retention of good performers in one location. They also need to be discussed in a recognized forum. The required number of people can be difficult to estimate. A human resources director responsible for coordinating succession planning in a multinational electronics company showed me an organization chart with present senior occupants and a name beneath each. Suitably impressed that something was being done, I was then told that this was only the start. The director said that what was needed was four names under each position. The rationale was as follows: one will leave, another will not be suitable, a third might not want it and the fourth will be left to fill the vacancy. All four will therefore need to be developed.

This attitude, born of experience and foresight, is consistent with what is happening in some organizations today. Succession planning depends on a careful appraisal of current and future business or operational needs that, as has been shown earlier, are subject to many pressures and can change and develop at very short notice. Therefore position, people or both can alter – even disappear – over a few years, depending on the business. Some markets, such as fashion in retail chains or the leisure and entertainment industry, can grow or contract rapidly and product life cycles are tending to be shorter anyway. That is why some firms have a succession development committee.[16]

> They comprise senior business and functional managers and usually the chief executive. They are serviced by the personnel specialist responsible for succession planning . . . They are an important forum for discussing and negotiating such moves (of managers out of the senior managers' territories).

Succession planning and, by implication, career development cannot be too long term or rely on developing only a few key people. As recent research has shown[17]

> There are no very reliable methods for examining skill needs in the future.

Recruiting young managers with potential for 15 years ahead may also not be a cost-effective approach, not only for the reasons mentioned above but also because career aspirations may change.

Different approaches to succession strategies

Recognizing some of these problems, companies may need to rethink their succession strategies according to their business needs. Four approaches illustrating this[18] are that of the:

- mature single business, such as IBM
- young single business, such as Amstrad
- diversified company strategic planning control, such as BAT Industries
- diversified company, financial control strategy, such as Hanson Plc.

The succession strategy for each is then analysed according to the type of executive required, the succession systems in operation and how the whole process is combined to deliver the strategy. The point here is that it is unnecessary to attempt to implement, say, an IBM system in a company such as BAT. The former depends on its complicated computer-based matching system, designed to meet a need for an international group of executives promoted from within and who have a detailed knowledge of the company's markets and products. The latter, it is suggested, needs executives to run different businesses, often acquired, in different sectors and that vary in maturity. There, the need is for executives capable of moving across businesses. Succession strategies can thus range from the highly planned to the more spontaneous, which are often found in young, fast-growing companies. The implications of these strategies will feed into career development and training. However, in order for them to work, they need some form of database from which to access suitable candidates.

2.12 Databases and talent banks

It follows that if succession strategies in companies need to be closely tailored to the business needs of the organization, similar focusing and flexibility will need to operate in the pool below senior executive level. Often, attention is only paid to this group when a crisis arises, such as when strategy is out of step with its implementation. For example, a company that had been producing integrated circuits required a multi-disciplinary type of engineer (computing, chemical, electrical and mechanical) to service the design, delivery and maintenance of the manufacturing systems. While having company-wide selection procedures, it had no ready access to data about an individual's training and experience. This information was urgently needed to decide whether there were enough potential trainees from inside to create staff for this area with the right mix of skills. In the meantime, a search was instigated externally and there was a delay of over nine months before the problem was resolved. Similarly, a large consultancy often had a need to field consultants with particular industrial sector experience or skills (languages). However, although all CVs were already on the database as complete documents, no method had been designed to codify the required information so that it could be retrieved selectively.

Information management

Clearly the problem is not one of availability of information but of information management: deciding which data to store in what categories and how to update and maintain them. For example, some organizations may keep an experience matrix[19] for each individual. This can take the form of different functional experience (finance, production and so on) cross-referenced by the type of unit or location in which it was acquired (overseas, head office, a particular location and so on). Incomplete cells in the matrix may serve as a useful reminder for discussion for both the organization and the individual. Another way might be to record key learning derived from the move. This could be policy making, general business knowledge, specialist experience or whatever the organization thinks is important. It has been argued[20] that company personnel information systems will be vital to the management of staff if organizations are to become more flexible and to obtain the benefits of functional, numerical and financial flexibility in their use of staff. Otherwise, companies could be drawn into short-term reactions such as over-recruiting or severe cutbacks that could be counter-productive. The personnel information system would need to distinguish who were 'core' and 'peripheral' workers and on what criteria they had been selected. The latter could be jobs, type of contract and pay, qualifications, skills, training received and mobility, to name but a few.

Talent banks

An interesting development is the maintenance of a company 'talent bank' used by a major hotel group whose policy is to promote people from within. The data collection is driven by the results of the appraisal system. For example, this would include what recommendations had been made for a particular person, what is likely to happen to him or her in six months or two years. Individuals (who are advised of this information and may have access to it on request) are given every opportunity to succeed through training and development. Career aspirations and other details are also recorded.

A factor that influences the success of the system is that there is a very low turnover of managers (though opportunities exist in sectors such as leisure, retailing and industrial catering). The managers are said to stay because they believe career opportunities exist for them and that their personal preferences are recorded and considered when any decisions are made about their careers.

2.13 Roles and accountabilities for careers

While human resource planning, succession planning, databases and talent banks have as their main focus the identification and provision of ways to meet the employment needs of the organization as a whole, career planning takes as its starting point the needs of the individual. The interface between the two is the line manager. It is helpful to think of the roles in career development in three broad categories:

– the organization – human resource management function and the board
– the line managers
– the individual.

Each has a part to play in ensuring that the appropriate information can be brought together and acted upon in career development.

Human resources department

The human resources function are custodians of certain organizational policies and processes that feed into career development, such as appraisal, remuneration and training. They can also provide access to certain career information and tools and decide whether all or some will be made available on a company-wide or restricted basis. Information about vacancies, assessment centres (for promotability), development centres (for self-awareness and career planning), counselling and special development programmes (such as converting specialists into line managers), are some of the options open to them.

Other options for career overseeing

Some large organizations such as NatWest bank have a centralized unit dedicated to career development using complex computerized recording and assessment systems. Others have a more diffuse function. The BBC recently advertised for a career development adviser whose role was to provide professional advice to line managers and human resources staff and provide them with the training and resources to offer a career development service to staff. There, the effort and focus was clearly devolved. Another variant may be that the board or executive committee take responsibility for the cadre of senior managers below them, the next layer down in the concern of the (group) head of management development or the head of an operating division and junior and middle management is the level that their line managers are expected to help to progress. This function may be formalized in the line managers' own appraisal.

Those involved in career development may still need to market their services to the rest of the organization as there can be a lack of understanding and problems of credibility of what the process as a whole can achieve. There are still attitudes to overcome, such as 'cream rises to the top' and a belief in the 'survival of the fittest', especially from those who think their success is due to their own efforts. Such individuals make it difficult for themselves and for their staff if they wish to approach and discuss their situation with someone who, in their view, has not held a managerial job.

The board

The organization is also represented by the board and the success of career development is closely affected by the degree of interest it takes. For example, one medium-sized company runs a modular senior executive programme open to all managers. The managing director chairs the selection panel, vetting its decisions and discussing them with the local directors and the management development function. This way, strategic needs of the company are kept to the forefront of any decisions and the human resources function understands the thinking of those who run the business. Finally, the visible support of the board for any career-related initiatives (such as secondments or new ventures) underlines the importance attached to career development and helps to coordinate activities across the organization. This is especially true for those that could provide opportunities to test executives as part of a carefully considered plan.

General managers

General managers can play a particularly important role here as they have the total picture of their own profit or cost centre as well as access to information about opportunities elsewhere. They will be informed about the wider organizational strategy because their unit will contribute to it and will be able to suggest career paths to their staff to consider on a longer-term basis, thus widening their horizons. In the short term, they are better able to select particular challenges for their managers and to offer feedback as part of the learning process.

Managers

Companies often use a shorthand phrase such as 'we develop our managers' when what they really mean is 'we help our managers to develop themselves'. While the business needs can offer the occasions for testing and senior managers prepare the individual, allocate work and give support, only the manager concerned can accept the challenges offered, deciding to learn and grow from them in relation to perceived internal needs.

2.14 Business needs and development assignments

A major way in which the organization can facilitate personal growth is through the provision of assignments. One study of nearly 200 successful executives aged in their early to middle forties reports 600 development experiences in their careers that made 'lasting changes in the way they manage'.[21] The authors categorized the assignments as:

– special projects and task forces
– start-ups
– fix-its
– leap in scope.

Special projects

Special projects (such as working as part of an acquisitions team) were within the staff rather than the line functions, through which the executives had risen to their present positions. They provided several key general lessons:

– learning how to handle their own ignorance about the topic under consideration
– getting others to cooperate without having any authority over them
– learning to cope with ambiguity (problems were conceptual or strategic and performance was therefore less easily measurable)
– an understanding of corporate strategy and culture.

Start-ups

The challenge of start-ups was to create something where nothing existed before, such as new products, markets, manufacturing plants, organizations and so on, and often having to create an entirely new staff. The lessons learned here were:

- identifying priorities
- motivating staff
- survival in adversity, with resulting self-confidence and willingness to take risks
- experiencing the loneliness of the leadership role.

Feedback was direct as managers had left behind something lasting and were directly accountable for the results.

Fix-its

Fix-its, or, turning a business around were a common form of development. Cash flows had to be restored, systems reviewed and replaced, product lines rationalized, plants closed, all against a deadline and perhaps strong organizational inertia or opposition.

Visibility was, by definition, high. The lessons here were tough decision making, often about people. This required them to develop contradictory attitudes and behaviour, such as being thick-skinned or sensitive according to the demands of the situation.

Unlike the start-up situation, the manager had the history and culture of the organization to overcome before being able to build anew.

Leap in scope

The leap in scope assignment was something wider and different to anything that had been learned before. Promotion could be within the same area or to a different one. The major lessons here were having to delegate, thereby risking finding mistakes or lack of efficiency, and clearing the way for others to let them get on with their jobs. Ensuring the success of others was their yardstick of success.

Conclusion

The study showed that assignments dealing with unexpected changes or which made demands on skills that the managers did not then have were most important for development. The authors concluded that 'shocks and pressures and problems with other people are the best teachers'. However, assignments need to be carefully thought out. This involves both the individual and the manager agreeing on the various targetted activities or skills that need improvement and seeing whether a proposed assignment would provide for some or all of their development. Otherwise it will not have the immediacy and relevance to the individuals' career.

The type of development assignment possible depends on the nature of the business and the company culture. A company in a stable environment would not encourage or provide risky assignments as they would seem irrelevant to the success of the organization.

2.15 Career development of senior executives

Recent research[22] on 144 directors from over 40 acknowledged blue chip companies showed that most directors learned accidentally and through unstructured experiences. Few had career objectives and a plan to help them achieve them. It seems that up until recently this *laissez-faire* policy has satisfied the business demands of organizations, but for how much longer?

It is not unusual for those involved in the development of senior executives to receive urgent requests for help as new responsibilities are taken on at home or abroad and gaps in knowledge need to be plugged quickly. Buying in expertise to bolster self-confidence and provide a quick method of gathering new ideas and concepts is essentially a short-term remedy. This is because managers may still be operating with old assumptions and frameworks and therefore find this new information difficult to absorb. Worse still, they may apply the hastily gained knowledge inappropriately in new situations.

Why should these findings matter? First, since directors set the strategic path of the organization, by implication they determine the human resources necessary to implement that strategy. Second, they provide the role model for the next layer of managers beneath them. If their attitude is that career development was unnecessary for *them* they will not support it for the next tier below.

2.16 Conclusion

This chapter has shown how environmental pressures are driving changes in the notion of 'career'. They are leading to a need to reassess the working relationship between individuals and organizations and also the satisfactions for both parties in that arrangement. The corporate response (what the organization sees, understands and chooses to act upon) in relation to those career drivers is determined by its business needs, past history, size, technology and culture.

Senior managers can help to align these two broad areas by being brokers of career opportunities for the individual and the organization. To do this they need information gathered from different levels in the organization and from formal and informal sources. The need goes beyond the basic and necessary biographical and appraisal information about individuals or organizational strategies. General managers have to recognize and understand the organizational challenges presented by having to facilitate managerial careers and deal with the associated problems. The subtle organizational processes and policies they have to master and operate within in order to find solutions will condition the extent of their own career success. These constraints will also affect their chances of contributing to their managers' ability to deal with their own careers.

In the turbulence and readjustment process generated by the environment, there is a potential danger for both the individual (less security of employment) and the organization (reduced employee commitment).

The new security, it is said, will come from being *employable* rather than being *employed*.[23] It will mean updating knowledge, skills and relevant experience as well as learning new modes of operation. The impetus for this needs to come from both parties: the organization will enhance its ability to recruit and retain staff by providing learning opportunities; the individual will be secure in the knowledge that current experience and skills will be valued by the organization and by the next employer. Continued enhancement of skills and abilities will therefore be the way of carving out a career in times of change. General managers and their staff will need to consult and negotiate more in adding pieces to the jigsaw of developing future managerial careers.

Applied questions

SENIOR MANAGERS

To what extent are the environmental career drivers affecting careers in your organization?
Are some of these more influential than others?
What is the corporate response to these?

MANAGERS

Do senior managers see themselves as having to provide developmental opportunities for you?
Are you aware of any databases and talent banks in your organization?
What information about you is held there? Will you have some input in what is stored?

HUMAN RESOURCE SPECIALISTS

Can you see new changes taking place and new organizational forms beginning to appear?

Are you having to adjust existing policies or create new ones to accommodate them?

Are you sure that your senior managers' responses to the environmental changes are taking into account the human resource planning implications?

References

1. Institute of Manpower Studies, *The Underutilization of Women in the Labour Force*, IMS, 1989.
2. National Economic Development Office, *Defusing the Demographic Time Bomb*, NEDO, 1989.
3. Curnow, B., 'Recruit, Retrain, Retain: Personnel Management and the Three r's', *Personnel Management*, November 1989.
4. Atkinson, J., 'Four Stages of Adjustment to the Demographic Downturn', *Personnel Management*, August 1989.
5. Drucker, P., *The New Realities*, Heineman, 1989.
6. Drucker, P., op. cit.
7. Atkinson, J., 'The Changing Corporation' in D. Clutterbuck (ed), *New Patterns of Work*, Gower, 1985.
8. Handy, C., *The Age of Unreason*, Hutchinson, 1989.
9. Lessem, R., 'The Enabling Company', in D. Clutterbuck (ed), *New Patterns of Work*, Gower, 1985.
10. Moss Kanter, R., *When Giants Learn to Dance*, Simon & Schuster, 1989.
11. Paul, N., and A. Warfield, 'The Impact of Divorce on Work', *Personnel Management*, February 1990.
12. Schein, E., *Career Dynamics*, Addison Wesley, 1977.
13. Schein, E., op. cit.
14. Purcell, J., 'The Impact of Corporate Strategy on Human Resource Management' in J. Storey (ed), *New Perspectives on Human Resource Management*, Routledge, 1989.
15. Gunz, H., 'Organizational Logics of Managerial Careers', *Organization Studies*, Vol. 9, No. 4, 1988.
16. Hirsch, W., *Succession Planning: Current practices and future issues*, IMS Report 184, Institute of Manpower Studies, 1990.
17. Hirsch, W., op. cit.
18. Gratton, L., and M. Syrett 'Heirs Apparent: Succession strategies for the future', *Personnel Management*, January 1990.
19. Hirsch, W., op. cit.
20. Richards-Carpenter, C., 'Proper Planning Demands Good Information', *Personnel Management*, April, 1983.
21. McCall, Jnr, M., M. Lombardo and A. Morrison, 'Great Leaps in Career Development' *Across the Board*, March 1989.
22. Mumford, A., G. Robinson and D. Stradling, *Developing Directors*, Manpower Services Commission/IMCB, 1989.
23. Moss Kanter, R., op.cit.

3
Organizational challenges: facilitating managers' careers

3.1 Introduction

The environmental pressures and the corporate response to them outlined in the previous chapter create a number of organizational challenges for senior managers. They can be brokers of career opportunities and, as such, have a fine balance to strike in meeting the needs of their board and those of their managers. Increasingly, general managers may discover that their staff, while performing well, find themselves in situations where they do not find it easy to comply with the organizations' expectations about their career. For example, moving into a new job that may be more administrative than technical; being socialized into a marketing rather than a financial role where the values and time scales are dissimilar; accepting a promotion; being mobile; balancing the perhaps conflicting demands of being in a dual career family; or being in a minority group. It is precisely in these kinds of areas that the general manager needs to be sensitive and creative in facilitating mutually acceptable solutions. This chapter aims to highlight these issues and present ways of dealing with them.

3.2 Enabling career transitions

The stresses of changing jobs

Changing from one job to another carries its own anxieties that, in turn, can affect performance. From a managerial viewpoint it is therefore worth monitoring a subordinates' method of dealing with the transition period as this can make or break future success. To understand this process, the different functions that being in a job involves need to be noted.

In general, the reasons for people working[1] are:

- economic returns, a means to other ends
- relating self to society
- status and self-respect
- meeting others
- personal identity
- passing time
- warding off distress
- personal achievement
- testing personal competence.

In any job, people will achieve their own relative balance of these needs. To change direction carries the potential threat of disturbing the balance, along with the feelings and behaviours that cluster around and reinforce the individual pattern.

Transitions occur within organizations when managers move vertically or horizontally into jobs or are placed in a situation that is a test of their competence. For example, a 45-year-old manager was moved from a factory-based management services job. He had spent all his previous career in a cost-cutting role in production environments within the same company. He was now to lead a centralized internal consultancy, working with clients in commercial as well as manufacturing divisions. The old job provided immediate status and self-respect and an opportunity to socialize with others after hours through factory-based functions. Time was spent in a familiar culture with a close knit community, although the factory employed over a thousand staff. The new situation upset this balance for several months. Status and respect were not immediately forthcoming from either internal staff or external clients. They had to be won, assignment by assignment. His authority was often severely questioned as clients had the last say. There were no established routines or social gatherings to ward off discomfort and personal competence was threatened. He initially made attempts at consultation with his well-qualified staff, which soon revealed themselves to be little more than 'brain picking' sessions. These were to acquire vicarious knowledge and experience with which to impress his new clients. Since no action ever followed these discussions, several consultants left or transferred to another part of the company. Then the economic climate changed for the worse and the function became closely led by requests from the board rather than by those from internal clients. The head of consultancy could now reapply old cost-cutting techniques rather than the new consultancy skills with which he had never been comfortable. The transition was made through a set of circumstances that suited the head and therefore the old work balance was almost restored.

Transitions involve three main processes:

- losing the old, familiar world
- searching for a new one
- a working through of the emotional effects on those left behind.

This latter area is a form of survivors' guilt. A well-qualified young man in his early thirties (a physics graduate with a PhD and experience in operations research) was moved from an advisory position in a management services function in the south of England. The new job in the north was production director for the manufacture of optical discs, then a new and difficult technological process. The old familiar world of long-term thinking was replaced by dealing with immediate crises in production. In the past, difficulties could always be resolved by using able colleagues from different disciplines as sounding boards. Decision making was a controlled and relaxed process with no final accountability. Naturally, attempts were made to cling to some of those comforting processes. Ex-colleagues were frequently invited to the factory to give social as well as technical support, as pressure could not be reduced by taking time off to visit a client. The former humorous behaviour could not now be used as an outlet for tension. In his search for new ways of doing things, the new director 'discovered' the telephone as a way to enlist support: 'Three phone calls, each with a name to contact, and I can get the right person to talk to across the world'. Confidence also grew in the internal resources available as he learned the art of management by walking about. Those left behind felt deprived of a good colleague intellectually and socially in both working and non-working hours. At the same time the move reminded them that they would have to make a similar transition in the not too distant future.

However able and competent managers are, they are likely to experience some problems, failures and frustrations during transition as they relearn how to perform effectively in organizations. All this takes time and survival needs support and practical help. One way of viewing this is as a transition curve (see Figure 3.1) that relates to managerial work.[2] The implications of this are presented in a useful summary,[3] an outline of which is given here.

The first phase is acclimatization. In the previous job the manager would have felt confident and competence there would have been high. Then, in the new position, effectiveness begins to decline slightly as peoples' assistance is sought, information is asked for and admissions are made of 'being new around here'. These cues generally signal to others not to hand the newcomer overly difficult jobs that may result in failure. Pointers are provided as to who the significant people are and tips offered freely to prevent social and technical pitfalls. Effectiveness may then increase back to former levels as the manager may wrongly conclude that

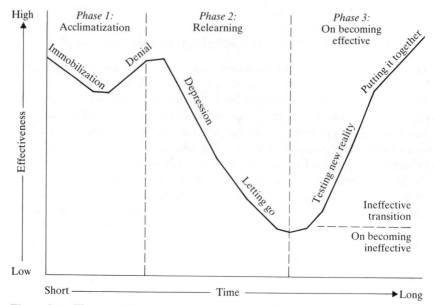

Figure 3.1 The transition curve
Source: Adapted, with permission, from Kakabadse, A., *The Politics of Management*, Gower Publishing Company Limited, Aldershot, 1983.

all past behaviour and attitudes are still appropriate and there is no real need to change. The test then appears in phase two where relearning has to take place. This need is usually prompted by the demands of others that the manager does a real job and pulls his or her weight as part of a team that may itself be under pressure. Mistakes or social blunders can occur resulting in disappointing and yet visible performance, followed by loss of confidence and depression. It is at this point that the individual realizes that attitudes must be changed, new skills learned and the personal image in the organization changed to raise performance. Phase three therefore involves constructing a new reality with new approaches to problems and seeking opportunities to test them. The individuals' speed of adjustment varies greatly. The transition process can take up to 18 months for some managers and even up to 4 years for others.

Why should this situation exist and for so long? Possible reasons[4] are:

– *inaccurate information*: there may be collusion by both recruiters and managers to sell the positive or strong points that each has to offer
– *unrealistic expectations*: there may be strong but unfulfilled needs on both sides and so the ideal picture that each has is knowingly compro-

mised, for example, the organization has to fill the vacancy at all costs and the individual cannot wait for another job

- *the image of the organization*: outwardly valuing certain attitudes or abilities such as entrepreneurialism and risk taking and then not allowing them to be used
- *lack of information about the future*: no clearly communicated strategy so that an individual can see where niche openings are in the next year or two.

3.3 Socialization of managers

As the previous section has shown, career transitions are a difficult stage for both organizations and individuals since there is always an element of risk involved at the outset. The risk can be considerably reduced if attention is paid by both parties to the socialization process. This can affect output and commitment to the job in question and prevent detachment from other people.

A key skill in making effective transitions and becoming a member of the new job group is sensitivity to the cues in the workplace that cannot be gleaned from job descriptions and lists of competences. Ways in which managers reduce the uncertainty are:

- changing peoples' expectations of the role
- finding acceptable ways of meeting conflicting demands made by others on their time and resources
- becoming part of the grapevine.

Newcomers also need to find out the norms of the work group and organization (the range of acceptable behaviour and whether they can operate at the limits). Positive and negative sanctions are identified as a result of seeing what happens when people step out of line. All this may involve unlearning old behaviour and need a shock to the frame of reference for this to happen. In one large defence systems company new recruits were always given a theoretically impossible product to design and left with a morning to set out their thinking for discussion later on. The usual conclusions were that the company had it all wrong and elaborate arguments were advanced as to why this product could not be made. At the end of the presentations, the product was revealed in full working order. This experience left its mark on the recruits. They saw that they had to be willing to really search for applied solutions to problems.

In deciphering organizations during socialization, certain concepts[5] are useful in understanding the newcomers' way of thinking. They are to do with locating oneself in:

social space
social time.

Social space

In mapping social space, the newcomer needs to adopt others' perspectives to see the world through their eyes and learn how he or she is seen in relation to other people in terms of worth and bargaining power. This awareness grows continuously from all the small as well as large incidents in work life until an image is created that the recruit has mastered the job script. This is done by redefining some elements of the job or slavishly following custom and practice to signal that its importance has been understood. Only then will the newcomer be entrusted with the informal knowledge of how to deal with a particular boss or take acceptable shortcuts. Individuals 'normalize the setting'[6] by assessing how typical theirs' and others' behaviour is. One example quoted is the 'something unusual' and 'nothing unusual' categorization. Here managers can usually tell if something is going to happen if 'something unusual' cues are given out by top managements' behaviour. Examples of these can be close questioning on unusual topics or playing things close to the chest instead of being open. Finding out what is normal also applies to the bosses' behaviour and to the subordinates' adjustment to it: knowing when to back down or offer support and so on. Recruits also need to find out what the real work is (for example being 'out there getting business rather than completing administrative tasks' is the common battle cry of the salesman). As well as absorbing the total range of behaviour at work, a newcomer has to discover the possible reasons for things occuring in the first place and whether action is needed.

Social time

Social time is the way a person groups the events that occur which then provide milestones and mark the end of personally significant phases at work. Once a manager can create themes (finding connections between the past and the future) expectations may form about career progression. Self-imposed timetables emerge (for example, for stays in particular jobs, for gaining advancement and responsibility) that may or may not correspond with the organizational norms. For instance, partnerships in large accountancy firms are generally offered to managers between 32 and 35 years old and anxiety occurs in those who feel that they may be almost outside the limit. Some managers may develop a series of milestones stretching out 20 years ahead that cause disproportionate disappointment if not met.

Adequate socialization of staff by senior managers may help to set realistic limits on these timetables and offer reassurance on their interpretation. Taking a more short-term view, the way time is managed at work is also conditioned by organizational socialization. Bosses, peers and subordinates will indicate that events are communally accepted as urgent and important and what behaviour is permitted at certain levels. For example, refusing the boss's request may be unacceptable in a culture that grades time according to seniority of level in the heirarchy of its user rather than by its contribution to the execution of a particular task.

The three key agents in the socialization process (rated for both helpfulness and availability) are according to one study[7] peers, senior colleagues and bosses. The point here is that it is the day-to-day interactions that are important, not the formal induction processes and literature. On the other hand, the absence of these would be noted as unprofessional practice on the part of the organization. One newly qualified director of an IT division of a consultancy used all three sources to settle in. He had moved from being head of an international marketing function with a vendor of IT products and services. For the first three months he systematically worked through a list of internal contacts including subordinates. He always ended the discussion with, 'If you were in my shoes, what would be the first changes you would make immediately and in the longer term?'. In that way, he tapped all the main sources of relevant information at three organizational levels. He gleaned the values, norms and sanctions of the organization, learned about its language, rituals, myths and systems. He was permitted to ask the 'naive' questions and seek explanations because of his status as a newcomer. Such questioning has to be part of the critical period of learning and occur within an acceptable timescale. If the learning does not take part during that time period, it cannot be easily acquired in that way again. After three months, such behaviour is deemed unacceptable and incompatible with the role of a director, who is supposed to provide a strategic focus for the practice, not ask *others* what the direction should be.

The importance of socialization

Clearly not all individuals may be such self-starters and a general manager can be a readymade source of contacts for the newcomers who are to be initiated. If socialization in these early months is inadequate or inappropriate it can threaten future prospects. Unless managers are socialized they will be unlikely to detect and practise the even more subtle behaviour differentiating satisfactory and outstanding performance on the present job and indicating promotability into future ones. Assuming the manager is competent, promotion may rest on the less tangible qualities such as acceptability to clients, executive presence and judgement. Perceptions about these qualities are very sharp in the early period in an organization and can be developed by helpful senior managers, thus preparing them for *their* next career step.

3.4 Preparing others for promotion

Selecting a group for special development is one effective way of ensuring top management succession. Merely being told that one has potential gives a sense of achievement in advance of the event. Preparing others for promotion may be seen by general managers as a direct contribution to the bottom line of their own units. It could also be viewed as part of a wider contribution to the corporate good, on the assumption that others will be doing the same for them. Anticipatory socialization (behaving in the way of the group to which you aspire) is vital but how are managers able to acquire the attitudes and behaviours of their successful leaders?

Mentoring

One much publicized way is mentoring – a process where an older, more experienced manager will offer support, encouragement and advice to a younger person and enhance their career by developing his or her potential. It is not instructing (which focuses on particular tasks) or coaching (which is directed to achieving specific results on the job).

Mentoring relationships occur in various ways. Some arise spontaneously, while others are formalized by organizations as a means of ensuring a future pool of managerial talent. The formalized process typically involves the reporting manager (two grades above the protégé) in consultation with the immediate supervisor and the mentor who is outside the organizational unit but of a comparable job or title to the reporting manager. The relationships are coordinated by the centre (for example, by a career development management manager) or by the human resources department of a localized unit.

The purposes of such schemes are many, including:[8]

- high-flyer development
- general development of employees
- developing a particular culture after acquisition or restructuring

- accelerated management development in response to an unforeseen shortage
- regular succession planning
- stimulating the growth of creativity
- as part of an equal opportunities programme
- safeguarding investment in managerial or graduate trainees
- overseeing development for qualifications for professional bodies.

SETTING IT UP

To be successful, the expected benefits of such programmes need to be assessed in relation to their purposes and so require careful installation. Assignment of responsibilities, agreement of how outcomes and problems should be managed, allocation of resources all have to be determined in advance by senior managers. Then there is the education of both parties in their respective roles as mentoring is, by definition, outside formal appraisal, although it may have an input from it. Following this, is the matching of mentors and protégés and the setting of formal timetables for opportunities for feedback to supplement the informal contact.

PROBLEMS

The mentoring process requires sensitive senior management involvement as it is not without its difficulties:

- the mentor can be seen to have more influence than the reporting manager
- there can be unwarrented interference by the mentor
- jealousy may be felt by the protégé's peers
- misinterpretation by others of cross-gender mentoring can occur
- over-dependence by the protégé on the mentor can be a problem
- cloning can happen
- the protégé may be used as the mentor's pawn, a disposable resource if the project fails, or to empire build
- the protégé may expect the mentor to pull strings
- there can be unpredictable side-effects, such as mentor and protégé leaving for better jobs together
- mismatches of personalities are possible
- unrealistic expectations of the benefits can be held by mentor and protégé.

However, none of these individual problems is so great that it cannot be overcome. Some or all of these taken together could be more difficult to root out.

SUCCESS

This is a question of striking the right balance. Each partner can profit from the relationship. The mentor may obtain:

- new knowledge or skills to prevent obsolescence
- support for policy implementation or new ventures
- a way of absorbing extra work
- an appraisal of lower-level reactions to decisions.

The protégé may gain:

- an insight into the attitudes and values of top management
- an opportunity for visibility through presentations or conducting special assignments
- the chance to see top management in action
- advance warning about changes.

The role and activity of the mentor has been classified as working in two main areas: career functions and psychosocial functions.[9] The former involves sponsorship (putting forward the protégé for projects or vacancies), visibility (exposure to decision makers and their strategic thinking) and providing feedback. All this helps to assess and reduce the risks to the protégé's reputation, while providing insights into organizational politics. The latter role is where the sponsor acts as a role model and enhances feelings of the protégé's competence and self-worth. The protégé is also able to discuss freely any anxieties and use the mentor as a sounding board.

THE EFFECTS OF GENDER

Much research suggests that mentoring for women needs special attention, as women tend not to actively seek out men as mentors and men mentors may not select women protégés.

A commonly cited reason for the lack of active seeking is an assumption by women that competence is the prequisite for advancement. Another is that men as mentors can hurt a career through disguised sexual advances. In addition, women may not have the right strategies to obtain a mentor, even if they had access to informal settings frequented by men mentors. The high visibility of a few women in an organization makes the stress of potential failure very high and some women are not prepared to live with this. As to the question of romantic involvement, women often have to defend their advancement against discrediting attacks and innuendos.

Non-selection of women as protégés by men is thought to be due to women being thought of by them as wives and mothers. Also, it is said, the male mentor cannot identify with the female protégé as a younger version of himself – a very important factor in the bonding process.

If such a relationship is problematical, why do women not act as mentors to other women? First, there are not enough women even now in senior positions to be mentors. Second, they have less time available to be a mentor as they often are working harder then the men to maintain and further their own careers.

OTHER FACTORS

Finally, organizational and cultural variables may affect whether mentoring relationships are possible and how many there can be. Task- or project-based organizations that are bound together in work groups may be a more conducive environment for mentoring since they tend to have fewer layers. Also, some professions are more likely to use a master–apprentice type of relationship and could therefore be more receptive to the need for mentoring at different points in a career: accountancy, law, medicine and engineering are some of them. Organizations may consider changing their appraisal and reward systems to specifically include mentoring and encourage more opportunities for interaction between senior and middle management staff.

Whatever type of mentoring system is evolved, it needs commitment, time and nurturing from general managers and other parties in the organization. In some cases, because of the large numbers of managers potentially involved, an organization may outline the mentoring process and then leave it to occur spontaneously without attempting to monitor it. This is the tactic of one large clearing bank in the UK.

3.5 Managerial mobility

If the process of preparing managers has been successful, the next career stage will involve some kind of mobility, either functional or geographical. This may be required as part of a high-flyer development scheme to gain specialist or other experience, to fill skill gaps or to remotivate staff. In addition, restructuring of organizations, new technology and new ventures may all put pressure on individuals to move in order to keep a job at all. Two trends in managerial mobility stand out: it is increasing at a general level and it is not always easy to achieve if the move is involuntary.

Recent research in the area[10] points to a high and rising rate of mobility. Most managers can expect to change jobs at least once in three years and most will experience a change in function. At least half will be spiralling, having simultaneous functional and upward status transition. It was found that the job changes were mostly radical in that they were right out of a family of job titles and in to another employment sector rather than merely moving between similar types of organization. This means that completely new demands were being made on the manager, with the consequent need to develop new skills. The job movers adopting these radical changes tended to be younger, specialists, women, in newer industrial and occupational settings (for example in management services rather than in old, industrial sectors) and in the private sector. The career implications drawn were that the route to the top was to pass out of one's function and company.

The pluses and minuses

Job mobility has positive or negative associations depending on whether it is voluntary or involuntary. A theme in recent surveys is that it is not as easy as it once was to persuade managers to move. Long-distance commuting into London (an hour or more by train) is not uncommon and it is estimated that some 10 000 commute weekly from the North to London and the South East, with Peterborough, Derby, Northampton and beyond considered feasible starting points. The commuters are typically middle management and technical grades, middle-aged and tied to their home location by the wishes of their partners and the educational needs of their children. They are not paid highly enough to obtain reasonable housing in the South East and so choose to commute. They reportedly suffer fatigue and stress from the hours of travel on top of a demanding job but receive little support from their employers in terms of flexible starting and finishing times. Some organizations may be more helpful and provide external assistance with information or financial help that could mean employees move nearer to their work.

Reluctance to relocate has consequences that senior management could mitigate. First, relocation is often a reactive strategy to space or business problems and communicated as late as possible – usually to avoid negative reactions when, in fact, it does the reverse. This lack of broader organizational planning creates other problems. Unforeseen delays, moving at the wrong time, unsettled staff who do not concentrate on the job and feel under stress, managers expected to do their job as usual *and* cope with relocation, all add to the confusion. Key employees may refuse to move and, even if they are persuaded to do so, they may be poached if the move is to an area of high employment.

The main message for general managers here is to anticipate likely resistance and give staff as much time as possible to make their own plans.

Getting all the problems on the table early on can be helpful as the staff with them have a vested interest in solving them. Employers such as the Civil Service spend considerable effort in communicating about relocation and the new facilities, arranging coach trips during work time so that people can visit the area. Others may provide external assistance with information about facilities, schooling, housing and various temporary allowances for accommodation and help with house buying and the associated fees. If problems are experienced with getting managers to be mobile within the UK, then the general manager will need to handle the situation even more carefully if there is a need for staff to relocate abroad.

3.6 Expatriates

There is every reason for general managers to consider the issues involved in the careers of expatriates. We are likely to see a new 'brain drain' from the UK to Europe for reasons explained in Chapter 2. This situation is likely to get worse due to the heavy recruitment by the Japanese for their local operations in Europe.

Two contradictory trends are being reported by recruitment consultants and multinationals. Due to the absence of up-to-date and accurate information from national statistics, it is difficult to determine the whole picture. The available evidence comes from independent surveys, so sample sizes are inevitably small. First, as a result of organizational restructuring and decentralization, multinationals that used to be big employers of expatriates are now favouring a local recruitment policy. This is to ensure motivation and cultural acceptability of their managers. In contrast, many companies are now expanding into new markets. Increasing interest is being shown in Eastern European countries, while opportunities in the Middle East are declining. High growth areas are Asia and Australasia.

While the balance of openings provided by employers has changed, so has the motivation of managers. The 1970s and early 1980s saw opportunist attractions for very substantial financial gain. Now managerial interest is focused more closely on the chance to acquire experience that will enhance career and promotion prospects.

Reasons for overseas postings

Organizations that employ expatriates invest very substantially in them and therefore expect a high payoff. There are several key reasons why managers are sent on foreign assignments:

- to control an overseas site by interpreting company strategy and having bottom-line accountability or to put in a company strong man
- to develop an awareness of the relationship between HQ and the subsidiary, understanding each others' problems, values and deadlines
- for cadre development – multinationals may have a career circuit where it is vital that future national and functional heads have experience of other cultures, become acquainted with them and seek the support of an international network
- to transfer expertise, such as production methods, information systems, engineering and construction design and techniques
- to train local nationals to become independent, say, by cascading training through teams
- to provide direct help if no local expertise is available
- to increase internal lateral and upward mobility, thus stopping managers becoming too comfortable in a job, leading to promotion blocks
- to develop high-flyers by using it as, say, a test of initiative in managing an operation under difficult conditions.

For it to be a productive exercise, it is important that senior managers and their staff are quite clear which of these reasons apply to any one posting.

A recent survey[11] of 25 multinationals across 5 sectors and 5 countries distinguishes between different characteristics of expatriates. They may be posted as technical experts or managers, on short- or long-term jobs, on single or multiple postings, on developmental or senior assignments, or for corporate or divisional (product) reasons.

The survey also showed that the employment of expatriates varies with the size and structure and the sector in which it is located. Electronics, banking and petroleum were the main employers in terms of numbers, in contrast with the airlines and the food and drink industry.

Recruitment and employment practice vary considerably for such assignments. Companies show a preference for their own staff where managerial expertise is needed. In particular, this applies if the company is trying to implement a uniform policy or approach or it is a senior posting. Technical specialists, on the other hand, can be recruited externally if necessary. Out of 15 reasons for selecting expatriates, the top three cited were expertise, linguistic ability and family support. However, the rigour of the selection systems varied from having detailed personal knowledge of the candidate to computer-listed names and a selection panel.

Pay

Expatriates can be costly and their remuneration problematical. Costs are incurred in transferring from one country to another (living costs and allowances) and through company overheads in maintaining a specialist unit that monitors and deals with all expatriate matters.

Remuneration practice is also variable. With a home-country system, the base salary and allowances enable the expatriate to keep up his or her old lifestyle. This eases the return home once the assignment is completed. The host-country pay system assumes the local rate for the job and the comparable lifestyle. This may cause problems if the local rate is less than the home rate and the expatriate cannot save anything.

A third type of system is where many of the base living costs are taken care of (housing, car, etc.). Only the goods and services purchases equivalent is part of the wage packet. This avoids the ups and downs of living standards while staff are moving around. It also avoids commensurate reductions in salary being seen as demotion or mean behaviour on the part of the company.

Within the EC, we can expect to see even greater mobility. There will be a complete harmonization of social security systems, facilitating an interchange of executives among national companies, although pension schemes will operate on a national basis. The reason for this is that if senior managers move around Europe in their last, highly paid 15 years, the host country will not wish to support a foreigner in retirement. This is an especially daunting prospect with a trend to an ageing population in Europe.

Training

The time from appointment to actual transfer can be very short and often little training takes place.[12] Six techniques used are:

- *shadowing*: acting as the HQ link before moving or meeting expatriates, all difficult to organize
- *looksees*: visiting the site
- *informal briefings*: short meetings with the personnel specialists or returners, videos and books, which is the most common set of methods
- *overlap*: tours of duty coincide for a short while to allow handover but the logistics can be difficult and expensive
- *formal training courses*: specialist courses about the country are given by external providers, about living in the country, its laws and practices
- *linguistic training*.

Settling in

Adjustment can be difficult as conversations with managers who are seasoned travellers show. One manager being counselled on a development programme in the UK commented:

If you were cycling or driving from one end of the country to another you would have time to stop and chat and see differences along the way – by the time you arrive you have already made a series of small adjustments and it isn't all such a shock. Contrast this with air travel where everything is too quick. There is little time to adjust. Now I arrive in a country a day or two before my first meeting, see a film and buy a paper. I would send managers a week early for an important meeting to acclimatize. Many deals are lost soon after arrival.

The speed and type of adjustment required is something that senior managers can directly affect, reducing the possible strain on their staff. Seven variables reported to affect adjustment[13] are:

- distance from home
- country
- similarity of job level and content
- social support
- duration of stay
- perceived benefits and costs of the move
- volunteering.

A key reported finding was that the happiness of the spouse was by far the most important factor in adjustment. Women tend to feel more isolated than men, which then reduces the man's satisfaction. Also, the more cultural barriers there were, such as religion, language and socio-economic developement, the less was the experienced job satisfaction.

In a video made by Alcan and McGill University in Canada, wives of career expatriates discussed their feelings about their lives. While the husband had the routines of the office to serve as an anchor point and might not have felt the need to be fluent in the new language, the wife's routine had to change. She needed the foreign language so that she could shop, as everything was in different packaging and sizes. The everyday details of life that were formerly taken for granted became insuperable obstacles without elementary linguistic skills. Even the ethics could be perceived as dubious as some wives said that nothing could be done in some countries without an additional bribe. Even recovering your furniture from the customs officials could be difficult if you were not prepared to pay them extra. One woman cited the extreme loneliness she felt and found herself envying a family in a shack in Mexico City simply because they were all together. An attitude important in combating loneliness was to accept the need for friendship. The woman said:

> You shouldn't say 'I'm only here for two years, I won't get close to people'. You need people.

Each family was said to be more dependent on members of the family because the family has to replace the whole community in terms of support and nurturance. The indications are that failure rates, that is, when staff are brought home before time, are fewer than they were in the 1970s and have declined to less than 5 per cent.[12] Nevertheless, that is not to say that there is no stress involved.

Success of a posting

The success of a posting depends on how sensitive managers are to other cultures' ways of managing. Several examples[14] drawn from surveys and anecdotes are cited. First, a good manager needs the ability to communicate, thought 41 per cent of a British sample compared with 12 per cent of the French and 14 per cent of Germans. Of the Germans, 50 per cent thought that the most important characteristic to possess was competence, compared with 34 per cent of the British. When asked what a manager should be doing, 52 per cent of the French said controlling, compared with only 2 per cent of the British.

Not only do values differ, but style does as well. The French executives prefer to set goals and policies and know answers. They would never think of asking a subordinate what his goals were since, by definition, they are to implement what the boss has decided. Nor would French bosses admit ignorance of a point or substitute a subordinate with specialist knowledge to answer for them. Latin Europe places a high value on the manager being able to give precise answers to questions subordinates have about their work. Another stereotype is that the French obey the letter of the law but not the spirit while the reverse is said to apply to the Americans. The latter have an image of being very goal-oriented in meetings, whereas Continentals will expect to develop a relationship before getting down to business. These few examples illustrate some of the subtleties that must be noted if business is to be transacted in Europe.

It is harder, clearly, to adapt to customs and practices further afield, as in Japan and the Far East! Western culture is far more competitive and individualistic and rewards managers for being so. While some attention in the West is given to being a good team player, in Japan the ethos is much more collectivistic. Westerners cannot conclude a deal with an individual but must seek feedback from the whole group. This can never be provided quickly since everything must be talked through until everyone agrees. Whereas the Japanese see negotiating as the development of a relationship, Westerners are seen to be driving and legalistic in their bargaining, trying to bring it to a swift and definite conclusion.

Adjustment to overseas postings clearly has career implications that general managers therefore need to monitor carefully. A manager has to quickly assess the organization, expatriate colleagues and subordinates. If he (there are virtually no women) decides to change things on little information, it could be risky. The value of his actions might not be apparent to the locals or to HQ (who will only see that the locals have been upset). If he does nothing, he will be seen as cautious and lacking in initiative.

Coming home

When the time comes to return home, the exit can be as fraught as the entry into the new country. There may be delays as the home country tries to find suitable openings. Often an advisory post at HQ could be a buffer but, as was seen in Chapter 1, restructuring and decentralization have severely limited this option. There may be fewer openings or a replacement may have grown into the expatriate's old job and now does not want to move. Even if a job is found, there may be no promotion. Having been in charge of an operation or being used to greater responsibility, a home-based post can seem very restrictive. In some cases a high standard of living, with accommodation, domestic help, expense accounts and paid school fees can be a difficult financial deal to give up.

On the social and cultural side, one expatriate wife said:

> Coming back was the most difficult time because you have changed and your country has changed. You don't feel good straightaway. People deal with you as a foreigner.

Therefore, on return, networks have to be painstakingly rebuilt and social opportunities exploited. This may be an area in which senior managers can ensure that help is forthcoming.

What to think about before going

What then are the implications for the general manager? First, preparation is a must. As transfers abroad can come with little warning, the general manager has to seek specialist help regarding remuneration and training. The latter needs to be specific to the host country and to the sector or function. It should also deal with practicalities: office routines, linguistic matters and cultural nuances. One organization in the UK uses foreign nationals in role plays of business meetings so that the individual manager can see the effects of his or her behaviour. Training for wives is another requirement since they will bear the brunt of the move and the biggest adjustments.

Second, an introduction into an expatriate network is helpful. A foreign diplomat once said how lucky he and his colleagues were before transfers. After all the briefings were over:

> You could rely on the fact that you would have an instant circle of friends who knew where you would be located. They would provide support from day one and there would be other little touches to show that you were welcome: flowers in the new home, a present and a list of contacts.

Increasingly, firms are looking to outside agencies to provide these touches, even to the extent of sending their representatives to meet the manager at the airport.

Third, the expatriate needs links with home: newsletters, details of colleagues and the feeling that someone at HQ is thinking about re-entry and the family's interests. A big question is how organizations will deal with dual career couples when one is offered a posting and the other does not wish to go.

3.7 Dual career couples

Dual career couples are those where both partners work in an occupation (usually professional or managerial). Therefore there is commitment beyond the basic hours, a sense of need for personal development and both contribute to the economic maintenance of the household.

While there appear to be no national statisics, and organizations would be hard pressed to produce numbers, evidence suggests that the number of these couples will grow as more married women enter the labour market. A recent survey by the Confederation of British Industry[15] warns that companies will have to change some of their employment policies to avoid losing key employees. Of the 130 firms surveyed, half said that employees were refusing to relocate because of the potential discord with their partners and loss of income. One third said a move would damage their spouses' career, a particularly difficult argument to counter.

A study

In one of the earliest studies[16] it was shown that dual career families were neither peculiar nor of above average intelligence although they were competent and resourceful in how they tackled their situation. Therefore such a living pattern is not out of the reach of others.

Their lifestyle often drew criticism from family, friends and colleagues. This added to the strain of having to make their lifestyle work without the traditional sources of support. Nor were the couples ruthless types. Their efforts to achieve a productive and satisfying lifestyle was not at the expense of others or their children.

Their lifestyle evolved rather than was consciously chosen. A particular difficulty at that time was there was some strain because there were very few role models and therefore everything had to be worked out as difficulties arose.

Within the families certain characteristics were reported to apply to the backgrounds of the women. They tended to be from higher socio-economic groups, have mothers who worked (or who were frustrated by not being allowed to work), be only or first children who desired approval and felt pressure to achieve, came from small families and had a close relationship with a figure of strength, especially their fathers.

The most striking feature was a sense of economic or social insecurity in childhood through loss of income or some displacement that led to a strong wish to develop an independent earning capability. The men were close to their mothers, but not overly dependent on them, and this laid the foundation for an awareness of and responsiveness to their wives' aspirations.

The dual career couple situation was not without its dilemmas. A major one was sheer overload. There was no spare capacity to do extra things, little entertaining and no time for oneself. The couples had to work to create a leisure space for their children and often the routine backup was neglected – in particular, household maintenance.

A second dilemma was the question of whose standards were to be adopted: their own or those of their family and friends? Remarks such as, 'Of course, you won't mind when the baby doesn't recognize you' had to be parried. Families also experienced a conflict between the egalitarian values of their relationship and the more conventional stereotyped sex roles of those of their friends.

Personal and social identity was also put under threat: the man's 'breadwinner' role was seen to be diluted by the woman working and the woman's 'homemaking' role was reduced by the paid help, which cast her as uncaring and unmaternal.

A fourth dilemma was how to maintain a social network for the sake of the children. There was less time for the informal chatting and reciprocation of favours outside the family round of work and home routines.

Finally there were problems of 'role cycling', that is alternating the priority given to one partner's needs and the other taking on the necessary caring role. The main source of conflict was over time management: whose needs were more pressing to do overtime, postponing working on a dissertation to attend the spouse's work party or cutting short a meeting for the partner to attend a conference. Within the home, time dilemmas centered around maintaining the standards of the three E's: elegance, ease and economy. It seemed impossible to ever satisfy more than two criteria simultaneously. Within all these conflicts, the models for their resolution were not well established.

Dual career family patterns

These are more complex than were at first thought and have been classified in different ways:[17]

- *accommodators*: one partner changes or adapts their working pattern to fit the needs of the other; one is high in work commitment and low in family involvement and vice versa
- *adversaries*: both are very career-oriented and neither is prepared to reduce work commitment; discomfort is experienced if one partner is more successful than the other
- *allies*: careers take priority but there is no sense of rivalry; they leave space in their diaries to be together or both are committed to the family first
- *acrobats*: they wish to excell in their careers but place a high priority on family life

However, whatever the preferred pattern, there are implications about how flexibility can be achieved. Four options emerge from recent research:[18]

- *dual flexibility*: both partners have the ability to vary hours
- *asymmetrical flexibility*: one person can vary hours, the other cannot
- *concurrent working*: both work, but at different, nonoverlapping times
- *symmetrical inflexibility*: both work long, inflexible hours.

General managers may find it useful to make themselves aware of which staff are in these situations, especially if they are key managers. The latter may require extra advance warning of requirements to work late or to travel.

Effects on the man's career

The consequences of dual career arrangements for the man have been reported in an exploratory study[19] as:

- *self-determination*: he can leave his job if he is not happy, reject excessive overtime or relocation because he has the security of another income to fall back on temporarily and he might wish to start his own business

- *ambition*: while there was a reduced need to climb the hierarchy at all costs, ambition focused more on professional and internal standards of success and satisfaction
- *motivation*: this was said to increase as wives were a source of support and often provided ideas or inspiration
- *stress*: a working wife can *reduce* stress as men are able to say what they feel at work because the concern about security is reduced.

These findings have major implications about how staff can be motivated and what may drive their careers. Again, the onus is on general managers to maintain a keen interest in their staffs' circumstances.

Apart from the above professional consequences for the man, there are also personal ones. There was an increase in parenting as more time had been spent in routine and other care. This was also accompanied by an increase in doing household chores.

In the main, the men felt that their situation increased marital happiness by expanding the number of experiences the couple had in common and by avoiding excessive dependance on the husband.

Effects on the woman's career

Similarly, there were consequences for the woman. Professionally, she may not be taken as seriously or always be believed by putting her husband's needs first. There is also a fear that she will not be mobile and not conform to the male model of work, which is that a man should work long hours and put the company first. Childcare is assumed to be totally her responsibility and it is thought that her work will be disrupted to cope with any emergencies.

Personally, there are costs in that the woman still carries the bulk of the work of organizing the household routines and is the centre of the children's and the family's social networks. The quid pro quo services that women who are full-time wives and mothers can provide for each other is lacking: there is no spare capacity for baby-sitting, child transport, coping with illness and emergencies and giving and receiving support and information about the local community, such as schools, hospitals, facilities, leisure activities, courses for children in the holidays.

Sometimes there is an element of guilt and the appearance of the 'superwoman complex'. This occurs when the wife feels the need to equal or surpass the domestic skills of the full-time housewife. She can even be overly concerned about being with the children when the latter would, in fact, prefer to be with their own friends and have their parents in the background.

Advantages

Despite the stresses and strains, there are advantages to offset them. Reported gains in the relationship for dual career couples are:

- *an increased centrality of the relationship*, compensating for the loss of social supports
- *financial security*: it is unlikely that both would lose their jobs simultaneously and both can make considered career changes
- *an increased ability to plan*
- *a willingness to take risks*: one partner could be entrepreneurial if the other was secure
- *reduction in rivalry*: conflicting demands are settled by what would benefit the family as a whole
- *an emphasis on encouraging children*: enhancing their competence and independence as there is little stereotyping of sex roles
- *the children's pride in them for doing something difficult*.

Conclusion

There is no doubt that this lifestyle is not easy for couples and there are a number of actions that organizations can take. First, the situation needs recognition. There are certain times when pressures within the dual career family are high and when additional demands can create problems, as happens when a child is ill. Seminars inside the organization can raise the awareness of older managers who may not have had to face these problems. They would therefore enable domestic life to be a legitimate topic for discussion on the managerial agenda.

Flexibility in working hours, job sharing, part-time working and locational arrangements are an obvious help. So too are knowledge and skills inputs in time management, stress reduction and so on. Help in finding a comparable choice of job for the spouse during relocation is another method by which organizations may reduce resistance to mobility.

Providing a variety of benefits from which employees can choose is a third way to ease these problems. Some employers offer choices of routine childcare options, assistance with nursery support or home visits by company nursing or auxiliary staff if children or relatives are sick. Parental leave would be another option.

Organizations can also assist by varying career expectations to suit the demands of the dual career lifestyle. Time spent in a job or progress over career routes may be longer than expected because at certain times energy is directed to family needs. Lateral moves may be more appropriate and general managers should be alert to this. After a period of time, the situation may ease, in which case promotion may follow as anticipated, or, individuals may prefer to stay at that level but still make a professional contribution. In that case the compensation and benefits can be varied accordingly. For example, holiday entitlement, time off in lieu of overtime, contribution to workplace nurseries off site are some of the ways. Another option is a flexible working hours scheme where leave can be amassed for personal needs.

All these are potential ways of retaining commitment from a satisfactory performer.

In some international banks, couples may be living apart in Japan or San Francisco, Seoul and Munich. It should be possible for organizations to create a climate where it is acceptable to say a transfer will cause difficulty without harming career prospects and that the management will seek and consider an alternative solution.

Couples are becoming increasingly dependent on two incomes and relocation for one and the loss of income for the other can be devastating. A policy shift is beginning to occur as some 10 per cent of companies are said to be offering spouse employment assistance packages. This may include financial compensation and practical help in finding jobs in a new location.

It can be said that managing a member of a dual career family needs awareness, sensitivity and flexibility. Organizations could well start by conducting their own internal research to see how many of their employees are in this situation, what particular difficulties they experience, how, if at all, this affects their work performance and what can be done by both parties to make the most effective decision. It could well avoid apparent lack of cooperation and demotivation of managers at work, which general managers might face if they ignore the matter or discourage their staff from raising it. Indeed, the treatment of this topic has certain similarities to the question of meeting the needs of minority groups.

3.8 Minority groups

Minority groups in this section are taken to mean those groups who are under-represented in management. While the list could be endless, the two that will be covered here are women and racial groups. Apart from the obvious moral and human rights arguments concerning equality of opportunity, there are some practical reasons why general managers may take an interest.

First, a key answer to the demographic skills shortage, (see Chapter 2) has been seen by the government and many pundits to lie in more recruitment from these groups. Second, it is believed to be harmful to the economy if the potential from these groups is not harnessed. Third, the working environment is becoming litigious and organizations could come under increasing legal scrutiny for discrimination, not only in recruitment and selection but also in career development. In this latter area little has been done to alleviate the problem, which has not been widely researched.

Women

A survey of the membership of the British Institute of Management[20] confirmed what most would suspect: that although women are found in all areas of management they are scarce at top levels and on the board. Moreover, women are rare in such areas as production, chemistry, engineering and construction. Nevertheless, they are found in public relations, financial and technical services and in the sectors concerned with the caring professions.

The survey found that a career in management still means that while marriage and a family are supportive structures for men, they are obstacles for women. Many more women than before are foregoing marriage and family life for the sake of their careers. A key finding was that women managers also tended to follow different career paths compared to men. They were educated to higher levels, occupying specialist positions at every point in the hierarchy. They tended to move faster between jobs and made more radical changes, (spiralling up and out). They maintained this pattern more or less continuously throughout their careers. They were said to have high growth needs, were intrinsically motivated and self-directed. Their male counterparts were, by contrast, found to be more materialistic, goal-directed and status-oriented. The women saw themselves as discriminated against by organizational policies and made these radical moves upwards as a means of being less subject to prejudice.

BARRIERS TO PROMOTION

The reported invisible barriers to promotion have become known as the 'glass ceiling'.[21] It is described as a complicated fabric of management myths and values that prevent women from reaching the top.

Women's progress is said to be slowed because organizations force them to perform at higher levels, while still in a more junior position, as it is thought to be risky to promote women. Failure to reach the top is attributed more often to 'poor image' for women than it is for men, and to either being over or under ambitious. If the image is not culturally acceptable it may be here that the lack of a mentor or role model has its most serious impact. As we have seen, there are several barriers to women establishing cross-gender mentoring relationships. Let us look at this in more detail:[22]

- *lack of access to information networks*
- *tokenism*: being a highly visible representative of their group puts mentors off in case mistakes are made or the relationship fails
- *stereotypes*: not being tough enough emotionally, good performance seen as being due to special effort rather than the result of consistent natural ability, women are not task-oriented enough, women working excessively hard to dispel stereotypes only to be told that, as they are working at their limit, they would not be able to cope with a promotion
- *socialization*: females are subtly encouraged early on to develop certain traits, such as fear of success, risk aversion, conflict avoidance and lack of assertiveness
- *lack of a role model*: the need for achievement and power may therefore not be exercised and this may then be seen as lack of motivation
- *ineffective power base*: men are more direct in exercising their power by direct bargaining while womens' influence is said to be more indirect, emphasizing weakness and drawing on kindness to achieve their goals.

If any of these exist in organizations, it is not surprising that the glass ceiling is a real problem for women in management. Senior managers have it in their power to raise the general awareness of these difficulties and encourage their organizations to adopt employment policies that would alleviate the situation.

OVERCOMING BARRIERS TO PROMOTION

As an initial step, organizations – with the encouragement and support of their general managers – can monitor the application of their equal opportunities policies. The first stage in this is to collect the relevant statistics about numbers of women recruited in relation to the total number of applicants. This will show whether discrimination is occurring at the recruitment stage.

It is also necessary to collect data about the proportional distribution of women in various types of jobs and levels, the analysis of leaving rates and the reasons behind this. British Telecom is known to have carried out such a survey of 1000 women in executive jobs. Whereas men constituted

30 per cent of the work-force, only 15 per cent of women occupied the management grades and only 2 per cent of the senior management grades. The women reported that they did not have help with combining career and family and that their management styles were rejected.

Positive action needs to be taken in the areas felt to be holding back womens' careers: career break schemes, childcare and flexible working arrangements. The survey also recommended a general rethink of its equal opportunities scheme. Littlewoods is reported to have introduced an equal opportunities programme covering the improvement of recruitment and promotion practices, specific promotion targets for minority groups and equal opportunities training for men and women. The results are impressive. Over a three-year period, the numbers in junior management have risen by 80 per cent, in the middle ranks by 55 per cent and in the senior grades, fourfold.

Awareness-raising programmes can be used to highlight areas that contribute to the 'glass ceiling', for example, stereotyping and lack of mentors. This area is currently being addressed through the growth of courses about women in management.

Racial minorities

The kinds of problems described for women in management (such as stereotyping) also apply to racial minorities. Discrimination does not usually occur in isolation but is reinforced by a web of employment practices so that it becomes self-perpetuating. Potential applicants may not be in the information network for job vacancies, especially if they are second generation and cannot draw on the experience of their immigrant parents. Even where companies avoid discrimination in recruitment and advertising, promotions from within may not occur if companies recruit management grades from outside. Discrimination is more likely to happen, too, in highly fragmented organizations where personnel procedures may be less formal and checkable compared with those with centralized control.

The Commission for Racial Equality is advocating positive action programmes. This means that organizations should encourage disadvantaged groups to apply for jobs in which they are unrepresented or give them training to develop their potential and enable them to compete on equal terms. They believe that managers need to be made aware of and responsible for these programmes and asked to report on their efficacy. Selection procedures and criteria also have to be monitored for indirect discriminatory effects. For example, recruitment preferences for certain institutes of further and higher education may encourage a bias towards certain types of recruits. These may themselves have a disproportionately low intake of particular racial groups. In the meantime, the numbers of managers from racial minority backgrounds is so low that a representative of the CRE knows of no reported research on the progress of such minorities in organizations.

3.9 Conclusion

The challenges that are being posed by the career needs of today's diversified work-force are not ones that can be solved satisfactorily by the routine application of corporate policies. With the devolution of responsibilities to operational or localized units, general managers will be required to facilitate their managers' careers by negotiation about career requirements. They will then need to lobby on their behalf within their own organizations if they are to retain them. They will need to offer a portfolio of options that will suit the particular values, lifestyles and aspirations of their staff and, simultaneously, meet the requirements of their business needs. Sensitivity, flexibility and responsiveness will be needed to meet the career requirements of internationally minded and multicultural managers and the minority groups who can be expected to swell their numbers.

Applied questions

SENIOR MANAGERS

What thought have you given to the way you deal with the challenges mentioned in this chapter?
Have you considered obtaining some extra information or training to enhance your ability to deal with them?
Are you aware of your own managers' views on these areas?

MANAGERS

Have you thought about your experiences and preferences in relation to the issues mentioned in this chapter?
Could you have been given more help and encouragement by others in the organization?

HUMAN RESOURCE SPECIALISTS

Are you monitoring the organizational trends in some of the areas covered here? Do you need to adjust your policies, attitudes and procedures?

Have you a mentoring scheme in your organization? How do senior managers and staff react to it?

References

1. Sofer, C., *Men in Mid-Career*, Cambridge University Press, 1970
2. Kakabadse, A., *The Politics of Management*, Gower, 1983.
3. Kakabadse, A., R. Ludlow, L. Vinnicombe, *Working in Organizations*, Gower, 1987. With permission of Gower Publishing Company Ltd., Aldershot.
4. Schein, E., *Career Dynamics*, Addison Wesley, 1977.
5. van Maanen, J., *Organizational Careers: Some new perspectives*, John Wiley, 1977.
6. van Maanen, J., op. cit.
7. Lewis, M., B. Posner, G. Powell, 'The Availability and Helpfulness of Socialization Practices', *Personnel Psychology*, Vol. 36, 1983.
8. Collin, A., 'Mentoring', *ICT*, March/April 1988.
9. Kram, K., 'Phases of the Mentoring Relationship', *Academy of Management Journal*, Vol. 26, 1983.
10. Nicholson, N., and A. West, *Managerial Job Change: Men and women in transition*, Cambridge University Press, 1988.
11. Brewster, C., *The Management of Expatriates*, Cranfield School of Management, 1988.
12. Furnham, A., and S. Bochner, *Culture Shock*, Methuen, 1986.
13. Furnham, A., and S. Bochner, op. cit.
14. Brooklyn-Derr, C., *Managing the New Careerists*, Josey Bass, 1986.
15. Confederation of British Industry, *Spouses, Partners and Domestic Assignments*, Vol. 1, CBI, 1990.
16. Rapoport, R., and R. Rapoport, *Dual Career Families Re-examined*, Martin Robertson, 1976.
17. Hall, F. S., and D. T. Hall, *The Two Career Couple*, Addison Wesley, 1980.
18. Rosin, H., 'Consequences for Men of Dual Career Marriages: Implications for organizations', *Journal of Managerial Psychology*, Vol. 5, No. 1, 1990.
19. Rosin, H., op. cit.
20. Nicholson, N., and A. West, op cit.
21. Morrison, A., R. White, E. van Velsor, *Breaking the Glass Ceiling*, Addison Wesley, 1987.
22. Noe, R., 'Women and Mentoring', *Academy of Mangement Review*, Vol. 13, No. 1, 1988.

4

Organizational challenges: dealing with managers' career problems

4.1 Introduction

As a result of the changes and environmental pressures on careers outlined in Chapter 2 and the organizations' response to them, the general manager is faced with another kind of organizational challenge. Individual managers may be so affected by these changes that attempts to facilitate careers in a way acceptable to both parties becomes more difficult. The general manager is then faced with having to deal with specific career problems and ways of tackling them such as:

– plateaued managers
– rust out and burnout
– transfers within the organization
– transfers outside the organization
– sabbaticals
– counselling out
– retirement and the older manager
– executive leasing
– the manager's own role as counsellor.

Sometimes these problems are temporary and can be alleviated. On other occasions, there is no solution but separation from the organization. For a more complete understanding, many of these problems need to be set against the backcloth of stages in the adult life cycle.

Mid-career crisis

A point at which the career and life cycles often overlap is when people are in their late thirties or early forties (often called the mid-career crisis) when permanent commitments in each sphere have been made. The results of these choices start to be seen and the gap between aspirations and reality becomes marked. There is often a complete reassessment of both parts of the manager's life.

In the area of careers, final decisions are being made and questions are being asked:

- 'Do I want to climb further in the hierarchy?'
- 'Can I retain my professionalism when the organization wants my administrative and managerial skills instead?'
- 'Should I now give priority to my partners' career?'
- 'Can I do something radically different – commercialize my favourite hobby, for example?'
- 'Is the competition from younger people proving too strong?'

All these are just a few of the questions that start to surface with more intensity at this particular life and career stage. These problems, if not handled correctly, can lead to a decrement in organizational as well as individual performance. Morale can be lowered and discontent can spread. For these reasons, they deserve attention from management.

4.2 Plateaued managers

Plateaued managers are those who have reached a point in the organizational hierarchy at which they are unlikely to progress further. This situation can occur for many reasons: structural and demographic, delayering of the steps in the hierarchy, individual abilities and personal motivation.

Structural factors

Structural factors contribute to plateauing in a multitude of ways. These factors include the continuing decline of manufacturing operations, the reduction of the size of organizational head quarters' roles and the decentralization of support staff to the business units. All this, coupled with the post-war population bulge, means that many able people have nowhere to go vertically in the organization. Here is one example.

A product division director had continuously fought to keep open a factory manufacturing consumer electrical goods by ensuring that the development of new lines took place on site. Eventually the battle was lost and Alex, the 38-year-old departmental head of management services in charge of 30 staff, was moved into a central role at the same grade but without staff. After a short while, he found that the central jobs, too, were being cut. Three months later he was moved to a division manufacturing defence equipment and allocated a staff of three. That division was subsequently sold and he was given a choice of a job without prospects or being made redundant. He chose the former option.

Delayering

In parallel with the foregoing changes, the effects of the delayering of organizational hierarchies (made worse by fast-stream schemes and inflexible pay structures tied to promotion) have combined to produce a glut of plateaued managers.

Take the case of John. He was a 37-year-old engineer with a good Cambridge degree, commercial interests and a willingness to consider jobs that would develop him. Designated a fast-streamer, the company ran out of local postings (several of which had overidden the ambitions of other capable candidates) and eventually sent him abroad. Now that he has been trying to return for the last three years, the plateau that had always been kept at bay now looks permanent.

Ability

Competence factors include the lack of ability to learn new skills or attitudes, the burning out of creativity or simply that the level of incompetence has been reached, as happened with Bruce.

He was a 49-year-old senior sales manager for a range of video products, mainly television and rental services. With the advent of video cassette recorders, optical discs and video for use in security and other applications, he was out of his depth technically. Never a good analyser of information but having a good relationship with his sales force and customers, his services were retained but confined strictly to what he knew best and could do well. Both parties recognized and accepted the plateau.

Motivation

Last but not least, perhaps the most important factor in avoiding or succumbing to plateauing is personal motivation.

David was a bright operations research specialist who had successfully applied his problem solving skills to business. He had been approached by two directors of commercial units in a multinational to join their respective management teams. Liking the variety of the internal consultancy work he was then doing and having remained at the same grade for three years, he was given the choice of accepting one of these line jobs or leaving. His view was that he would not be able to adapt to the routines and confinement surrounding one job in one operation. To the disappointment of all concerned, he left.

Another example was Jane who, at 41, was a successful manager in a government department, advising the personnel division and ministers on specified legal matters and also drafting statutory instruments. Friendly and personable, she accepted that she could not go any further in the Civil Service and was locked into a role. She had passed quickly up the promotion ladder to assistant secretary level, but had had no managerial or other experience in commercial practice and so could not leave. She had seen this situation coming up but had not attempted to do anything about it, possibly because her husband had a job and she was able to divert some of her attention to his career.

Reactions to plateauing

People's reactions to plateauing can differ markedly and they have been classified as follows:[1]

- *contented maturity*: senior managers, 40+, with the company 10 or more years and usually graduates with technical knowledge and drive. Displaced by fast-track graduates, they will still remain as they have a sense of loyalty and work is not the only source of self-esteem
- *discontented maturity*: also 40+ and still keen to be promoted, they may show poor morale, over conservativism and cynicism and they often create inertia rather than the stability provided by their colleagues in the first category
- *thwarted rising stars*: aged around 35, these rising stars may now resent the lack of opportunity the firm can provide for them (these high expectations may have been fuelled by graduate training courses such as MBAs).

The key contrast for these people is the difference between having a great future and the recognition of lost opportunities and an underachieving past. All need careful monitoring and motivating if they are not to become disruptive. Even those in contented maturity can slip into the discontented mode if poorly managed.

Things for managers to note

It is crucial for the general manager to recognize that there may be some functions or parts of the organization that are more prone to having plateaued managers than others. Due to the specialists employed and/or the flat structure, there may be only three levels to director status, or immediately below.

Research and development, personnel and training, accounts and finance are some typical areas where help and attention may be needed in personal and career development.

Spotting the signs is a useful skill for senior managers to develop. Loss of motivation, psychosomatic illness, absenteeism and apathy are but a few.

The visible effects of mid-career crisis have been categorized as:[2]

- *psychological*: feelings of unexplained depression, frustration and boredom, resentment that 20 years may have been spent pursuing the wrong goals, loss of self-esteem as the age span in which one can become a star has passed, frantic attempts to keep up to date by calling in a series of external experts
- *physical*: fatigue, fitness obsession and body talk
- *family discord*: the frustration-aggression syndrome takes hold as the manager realizes the family has been neglected for a career; it is the only source of support but everyone now has separate interests and has learned to do without him or her
- *marital stress*: disappointment in career is often redirected to disappointment in a partner
- *colleague alienation*: the focus for this varies: a specific person or group, a generation, or a particular topic; vendattas are conducted to release psychological aggression and there is a denial of rewards to others, criticism, and gossip.

The result of all this can be the creation of an unpleasant work environment, reduced job performance and lowered morale, especially if there are new recruits. The latter may then start to acquire a scepticism without ever having had personal cause to do so.

Positive action

What options are there for dealing with this? At first sight the cynic might say, 'let them all go'. However, these people were once useful and maybe were designated as high-flyers. Many will be the solid citizens on whom the regular functioning of an organization depends.

Perhaps the first thing senior managers can do is help to create a set of values that does not equate success wholly with promotion but with self-development. They could allow that it is acceptable *not* to strive for promotion, so long as one is still contributing and developing. Appraisal and compensation systems that enforce the 'up or out' ethic can be damaging and emphasize unhealthy competition.

Second, it may be worth formally exploring how widespread plateauing is in the organization and talking to individuals about their perceived potential before problems arise.

Third, there may be opportunities for restructuring jobs to increase their scope and status. Jobs could play to particular strengths and interests of an individual so that he or she becomes the 'manager responsible for' or the 'company expert on' a particular area. This perhaps could be accompanied by changes in the remuneration system, using merit awards or a special duties allowance.

Fourth, some organizations run mid-career courses or workshops, typically lasting a day or two. These examine and reassess career goals, strengths and weaknesses, motivation and development needs and explore changes in direction.

The Civil Service, the Wellcome Foundation, Pedigree Petfoods and ICI are just a few firms reported to run courses internally for mid-career managers. Alternatively, help can be sought from outside. Participants usually find that such a programme enhances self-esteem, and helps them to provide specific goals and action plans for themselves. Other important options, such as transfers (internal and external) and sabbaticals, can benefit both the individual and the organization and are covered later in this chapter.

4.3 Rust out and burnout

Often related to, but not always synonymous with, the plateaued manager and mid-life crisis are the syndromes of rust out and burnout.[3] They can affect people of any age and are related to stress and performance.

Rust out

We all need a certain amount of stress otherwise, through understimulation, we are not motivated to perform. This is rust out.

People in this situation report lack of challenge, boredom, fatigue and depression. They turn 'rusty' through staying too long in the same job without periods of variety and change. The job may have become routine or so controlled by procedures or outside agents that responses become mechanical. There is no spur to grow and change, even when there are promotion opportunities.

Burnout

In complete contrast, there are managers who have been so stressed by requirements to perform that their ability to do so is now impaired by an *excess* of activity. They have become hard driving, aggressive and over-ambitious. They are the ones who work very long hours to get through their work, do not use their full leave entitlement, become inward-looking and obsessed with their tasks. Performance is impaired not only in the quantity of work able to be tackled but in the quality of decision making. Irrationality, stereotyping and tunnel vision may occur here.

Causes and solutions

The aim in these cases is to first examine the triggers and underlying causes associated with these extremes of behaviour. Company culture can play a part here. It can encourage the workaholic (a candidate for burnout) *and* the 'skiver' (or rusted out person) who has long given up trying to influence events.

Next, it is necessary to nudge the managers into the optimum stress zone, where they will be motivated, creative, rational, willing to learn and satisfied with what they are doing. If they stay at either extreme they will certainly be plateaued, if not fired.

The remedial action their bosses can take if their staff are rusted out is to provide an agreed structure for their job. Objectives and time scales and some variety of pace and duties need to be spelled out until these become internalized and act as motivators in their own right. People need to start to take risks to challenge their abilities, avoid isolation and to stretch for success. They need to feel part of the collective purpose of the organization.

For those at the burnout stage, rehabilitation may take longer. It involves reducing the stress load, also by a structured approach of prioritizing, time management, avoiding too much contact with people and learning to say 'no'.

4.4 Transfers within the organization

To overcome some of the problems posed by plateaued managers and those suffering from rust out and burnout, there are always other options of temporary work within the organization, with the express purpose of providing some novel experience, challenge or change of surroundings, can be useful. Special assignments, either alone or as part of a task force can meet these criteria. When a manager is part of a multidisciplinary team, distinctions such as age, grade and status, while not being entirely forgotten, are pushed more into the background by the importance, urgency and deadlines imposed by the task.

Merely doing a similar job in a different context can also be helpful. For example, in a building society or retail bank some managers may act as a relief to another branch to cover for illness or holidays. In the Civil Service and the police force, it is possible to be transferred to another department on a temporary basis. However, to be beneficial, clear objectives need to be set for the expected contribution of both parties, a means of appraisal agreed and a specific date for termination of the arrangement otherwise the experience may be devalued. The host department may believe that someone is being off-loaded and the transferee will feel isolated.

4.5 Transfers outside the organization

Short-term secondments

Temporary transfers outside the organization can also be beneficial to the seconding and receiving organizations. In the past, it may have only been associated with unblocking promotional routes. This was achieved by sending plateaued managers in banks and blue chip organizations to pass their time until retirement in charitable organizations in need of professional assistance. That image is now changing with companies like IBM and BP using secondments more positively. The Nationwide Anglia Building Society is reported as using secondments as part of a management development scheme.

In contrast with the old style, pre-retirement secondment, which would last about two years and not bring expertise back into the organization, these schemes are deliberately short. A typical time allocation and scale might be a day or two a week over a few months. At the end of the specified period, presentations were made by secondees to the host and to the lending organizations' senior management. Reported benefits were increased self-confidence and local marketing knowledge, as well as developments in completely new managerial disciplines.

Longer-term secondments

In contrast to the short-term secondments mentioned above, some can last two or three years and have a major career impact. Peter was a 42-year-old sales manager with a large blue chip company selling lighting and related products into the consumer, professional and specialist markets. Having been four years in the job, he had reached a point where there was no vertical promotion available at the time. Fortunately, the group wanted to take over a small specialist firm and gradually integrate it into the mainstream business. Peter was offered the chance to run the small company and become its managing director.

At first he had mixed feelings as he had only limited functional experience to offer. He accepted the posting and was exposed to pressures he had not experienced before. He then saw himself as remote from the customers (difficult for a former sales manager whose strength was customer relations) and had to cope with longer-term planning and administration, which he did not like. The pressure for overall financial results was considerable and felt all the more, since he had to manage other functions that he did not fully understand. The learning was direct and rapid and he attended numerous courses on finance, accounting, personnel management and marketing.

Three years later the company was formally drawn into the mainstream operation and Peter was promoted to divisional director to take charge of a large part of the business.

A particular point to note here is that this was a localized initiative of a particular business unit whose director took responsibility for turning the potential resignation of a good member of staff into a business success. A senior manager expressing confidence in what had seemed to be a plateaued manager provided a launch pad for growth.

Exchanges

The Civil Service, in an attempt to foster better relations with industry and commerce has been encouraging government and business exchanges. The reported intention on the part of the Civil Service is to enable better customer/supplier working relations and/or joint ventures. From the perspective of industry and commerce these reasons also apply and there are additional benefits if organizations are assessing the market for a new product or service.

One management consultancy sent one of its high-flyers to the Treasury to advise on financial control systems and other related initiatives. On his return he was promoted and later became the director responsible for the newly formed division dealing with the public sector.

Although the process has its benefits and enables the removal of stereotypes – in this case, the tea-drinking civil servant and the unprincipled businessman with perks – it is not without its difficulties. Disparities in remuneration have to be resolved and re-entry guarantees for staff vary. It is easier for the Civil Service to provide them because of its sheer size. Those in industry and commerce tend not to wish to be away too long in case future career opportunities are missed. The consequences of a failed placement are also potentially serious because of the high visibility of an outsider entering another organization and because of the likelihood of prejudicing the chances of future secondees. External secondments therefore need careful monitoring by general managers to ensure that they do not ultimately increase career frustration.

4.6 Sabbaticals

The practice of sabbaticals (extended periods of leave from one's employing organization) has long been used by academic institutions. Its purpose there is intellectual and creative rejuvenation and a means of rewarding valued staff. The duration can be variable but is not normally in excess of a year. At the end of this period, some tangible evidence of how the time has been spent is expected: a book, a report or expertise acquired in a new methodology. The idea is now spreading to industry and commerce and other organizations, both for remedial and other reasons. Reported exponents of this are Touche Ross, Scottish and Newcastle Breweries, Apple Computers and the John Lewis Partnership. The latter company is reported to put certain constraints on staff eligibility: age (older than 47 years) and, length of service (25 years), in order to qualify for 6 months' leave to do anything they wish.

Clearly, organizations will have different views on how the solution can be managed. It is becoming less likely, for example, that an organization will be able to insist on 25 years' service, given the way employment practices are changing. Organizations may also vary as to whether employees are given full pay and whether there is a guaranteed job at the end of it.

Companies may not always be willing to advertise the fact that they grant sabbaticals in case it becomes an area for bargaining or inclusion as part of an employment contract. They prefer to use it as a discretionary option either to reward staff or prevent rust out or burnout. Sabatticals offer a valuable chance to stand back and reconsider personal lives achievements and activities. Companies report that individuals usually return with new perspectives and a broader range of skills that can enhance their value to the organization. Other company justifications are that sabbaticals are part of a health care activity and, as such, are an investment in their effective use of human resources.

4.7 Counselling out

If attempts fail to revive the careers of plateaued or under-performing managers through temporary transfers in and outside the organization and sabbaticals, the only options left to the general manager are to counsel out, retire staff early (see 4.8) and encourage executive leasing.

The term counselling out has replaced 'making redundant' or giving 'the sack' for very good reasons. From the organizations' viewpoint, there is a need to avoid acquiring an image of a 'hire and fire' organization, as this adversely affects recruitment and client relations. They also wish to retain goodwill, since the employee may subsequently work for a supplier or customer. Ex-employees might have an indirect influence over some of the firms' activities and be in a position to affect its reputation. From the individual perspective, the environment may simply be the wrong one for his or her particular skills and values.

Counselling

Firms are increasingly recognizing that they have a responsibility for the well-being of their staff and a counselling service is often negotiated as part of the severance package. Firms that do this usually retain the service of specialist advisers (psychologists or outplacement agencies). While each firm of advisers has its own approach, a typical sequence might be as follows:

– *organizational briefing*: the counsellors attend formal meetings with its senior management to familiarize themselves with the business, the reasons behind the decisions and so on
– *counsellors attend the individual or group announcement*: to take the emotional impact and provide an emotional outlet for the negative feelings of those affected
– *a database of vacancies in other firms is set up*
– *individual needs are diagnosed*: occupational aptitude tests and personality questionnaires are used
– *counsellors discuss findings*: prospects are identified for the client
– *advice and training are given*: CV preparation, self-presentation, interview skills.

THE BENEFITS

Clearly, the value of all this depends as much on the receptivity of the individual as on the professionalism of the outplacement agency.

The counsellors are themselves trained to handle all the negative reactions to career failure and, in many cases, outplacement agencies like to recruit those who have themselves been made redundant. They can then empathize with what is happening in the client's mind.

Some common reactions to job loss can be a rationalization of events, saying 'it was bad management that put the company in a weak situation', or defence mechanisms designed to protect the individual from loss of self-esteem, saying things like, 'my boss couldn't recognize talent'. People can also turn inwards and punish themselves if they are not allowed to express their anger or can appear to deny the reality by emphasizing the importance of the non-work role – 'there is more to life than work'. All these issues should be identified and worked through with the client.

FACTORS THAT MAKE NEW EMPLOYMENT DIFFICULT

These outplacement agencies tend to charge about 15 per cent of the client's last salary and claim to have a good track record in finding people new employment (usually within three to four months of registration). Known users are BP, Morgan Grenfell, Caterpillar and Metal Box, to name but a few. The factors or personality types that singly or in combination raise the difficulty level of placement are, according to one source[4] being:

- *unemployed*
- *over 55*
- *stickers*: those who remained in one job for a long time or in one organization without any variety of executive experience
- *bouncers*: those where tenure in the last job was very short, as this affects their confidence and concerns the new employers
- *changers*: those who have had frequent job changes, which raises questions about commitment.

PSYCHOLOGICAL EFFECTS

Psychologically, for the individual it is another form of transition and relearning (see Chapter 3). The services of counselling provide major benefits for the individual client. At a time when individuals are recovering from the initial shock and anger, counselling makes them help themselves to move forward. It provides a structure when familiar routines of going to work have vanished overnight. Instead, the person maintains a routine of going to work in an office and having appointments to keep and tasks to complete for the counsellor, who can facilitate progress and can also provide contacts. The client has a desk, telephone, reference material, secretarial and technical support and can approach the situation like another task to be completed. The motivation is naturally very high.

Second, there is plenty of contact and moral support from others in a similar situation, which keeps up morale.

Third, there is a positive approach to restoring the clients' self-esteem. One candidate said:

> It was fantastic. On day one you are listing all your achievements in the last 20 years instead of thinking about failures. These are analysed for major themes and key words that have significance for how you approach the world.

Receiving feedback from batteries of intellectual, personality, motivational tests and inventories is also designed to build confidence.

Fourth, clients emerge much stronger from the experience when they accept that this is indeed the end of an old world but that it is *also* the beginning of a new one. Problems that come along now can be tackled as clients are in control of the decisions, having rethought their life, family and career goals.

Finally, they learn new techniques, (technical and social) and the ability to network.

The effects on the remaining employed

The general manager has to watch the effect of redundancy on those left behind. Often the first indication to them is an empty desk or being informed that the individual has had to leave at short notice because of the commercial sensitivity of the situation. There is no chance to say 'goodbye'. There is a mixture of feelings, such as a sense of loss and 'survivors' guilt'. A sense of relief that 'it's not me' and a little anxiety coexist with a questioning of where the organization is really going if it resorts to shedding people and whether it will continue to be successful.

4.8 Retirement and the older manager

Early retirement

Early retirement is another option for dealing with career problems of staff although it should not be interpreted as the end of paid employment.

A recent survey by the Institute of Personnel Management[5] covered 72 private sector companies, the majority having between 1000 and 25 000 employees. Over half the companies reported that there was an increase in the number of men taking early retirement while only 37 per cent saw the same trend among women employees. About 25 per cent of the companies said that they re-employed around 20 per cent of their male managers and supervisors who had taken early retirement. About half the companies predicted that there would be an increase in both male and female managers who would be thus re-employed over the next 10 years.

IBM has recently set up a company called Skillbase. It sells the expertise of early retirees (those 53 years old and above). They receive a year's salary and no reduction of pension. They are also guaranteed 90 days' work with IBM for 2 years after retirement at 40 per cent of their previous base salary. Their expertise is also sold to other companies and this external demand is increasing.

Retirement training

Lever Brothers (part of Unilever) has a comprehensive retirement training procedure that was started in the early 1980s, and so does Polaroid. The spur to the Lever Brothers' work[6] was the need to reduce staff numbers by 75 per cent over several years. Examination of the manpower planning information and age structure of the firm showed that what was needed was a culture that actively supported earlier retirement. The broad plan was to encourage individuals to question their own needs and attitudes while also reassuring them with information and expertise about financial provision. Staff were often young enough to consider alternative careers, which also needed planning.

The framework envisaged was that when a group was some 10 years away from retirement, a one-day seminar would be held to alert people to areas that they should be thinking about, especially the long-term financial aspects. Five years away, a two-day off-site course was held for managers and their partners so that they could be helped to make decisions together. A year off, there was a one-day seminar to make plans when examining detailed information about financial, personal and career prospects. Six months off, the working week would be gradually reduced to two days. Therefore, when retirement did come, managers had been carefully prepared. Afterwards, there was the option of continuity of support for part-time jobs and entry into networks of people who had built their own businesses.

The key philosophy around which the company had constructed their scheme was that retirement was a process, not a specific event. This shared understanding of management and staff alike made it easier to be integrated with business decisions.

The programme was managed and delivered by a core staff team of in-coming line and staff management. They acted as facilitators and enabled the pre-retirement group to share and work through their feelings. The aim was to encourage active growth and development rather than a resigned, passive acceptance. The process was one of empowerment so that individuals were not just receiving information but owning it and acting upon it in a way directed to their goals. They had to work on data files themselves (for example, retirement information and pension forecasts) and participated in a personal counselling process.

Senior managers are in a good position to know when business needs are likely to require a shedding of staff through natural wastage. They should therefore be able to alert their human resources departments to plan for suitable pre-retirement programmes.

4.9 Executive leasing

Another growing option for executives who, for whatever reason are leaving their employer, is executive leasing. This is where experienced managers are employed elsewhere on a temporary basis. A composite profile of such an executive would be that he or she was over 40 years old, an early retiree or freelance, self-motivated and flexible. These may also be people who are in career transition and do not want long-term commitment but do wish to extend their repertoire of activities. They are also versatile and can probably operate in a specialist or general management role.

Executive leasing is operated by a relatively small number of companies acting as agents. The benefits for their clients are access to a talented database of executives to provide skills 'on tap' when required. They can join the firm at short notice, avoiding the common delays of using search consultants and handing in notice. There are no recruitment or termination costs, either actual or hidden and new ideas can be brought in fast if the executive joins the management team. The firm is therefore able to achieve objectives that otherwise might not be possible. This is especially true for small or medium-sized companies who cannot afford staff in full-time or specialist roles.

Benefits

The great strength of this option is that the potential uses of such staff are many and varied:

– *handling excess volume of work*: teams overstretched through coping with too much change, seasonal peak handling; coping with illness and bridging succession
– *providing support*: helping organizations to grow or run down, managing non-mainstream activities, a new product or division, rescuing a department in trouble and preparing a department for change

– *innovation*: developing new products or services, providing a marketing plan, revitalizing a new operation and handling acquisitions by easing the acquired company into the mainstream.

It is precisely because of this potential variety of jobs that the experience can be rewarding and beneficial to both parties.

4.10 The manager as counsellor

So far, consideration here of the various problems and range of actions that can be taken has not touched on the possibility of the line manager also being a 'front-line' personal counsellor (actual company policies and schemes will be covered in Chapter 6). Indeed, general managers may feel that there might be a need, but are hesitant about tackling the personal issues that may be the cause or the context for many of the work problems. This may be because of one or more various beliefs about themselves or the process, including:

– lack of appropriate skills
– lack of time – counselling demands patience and energy
– people should be able to 'pull themselves together'
– diminution of the assessors' role (it is difficult for managers used to making evaluative comments about their staff to be objective and non-judgemental with the same staff but in a different situation)
– sympathy may be interpreted as a weakness, to be later exploited by staff
– expressed sympathy makes it difficult to make legitimate demands back in the job context.

These are all realistic concerns that need to be balanced against the possible payoff of removing the problems that reduce work performance.

Problems

There may also be a fear of making mistakes in an area where the manager cannot resort to their authority if things get out of control. In fact, some common mistakes (if no training has been given) are to try and help by giving advice, making statements that begin, 'If I were you . . .', or trying to cheer people up with 'Well, it won't last forever, will it?' At best this can appear insensitive and at worst it can start to be depressing by acting as a foil to the individual's misery.

Offering solutions is a particular temptation to senior managers who pride themselves on their problem solving ability, which they are then required to hold in check. Similarly, managers who are used to decision making want to get into the action phase straight away. Finally, it is all too easy to appear to try and empathize by reminiscing, saying things like 'I remember when I was in just the same situation', and then use the discussion to off-load one's own, unresolved problems.

Remedies through training

These fears and mistakes can be remedied by some training and reading. The phases of counselling can be classified in a number of ways, but a simple three-phase scheme[7] can be used to describe how the counsellor's and the client's (manager's) tasks can run in parallel:

Phase	Counsellor's task		Client's task
1	Understanding	leading to	defining the problem
2	Challenging	leading to	redefining the problem
3	Resourcing	leading to	managing the problem

In phase 1, the counsellor, by active listening, can develop rapport, begin to empathize and have enough detail to begin asking probing questions. The client during this stage may initially give complicated and confused accounts, talking about events in a random order and not being able to see the wood for the trees. As a result of being able to talk things through and with a little nudging from the counsellor, definition and ownership of the problem is reached.

During phase 2, the counsellor's role is to challenge, probe and ask hypothetical questions in a kind but firm way. The client in the meantime starts to redefine the problem by breaking it up into manageable pieces and gradually sees what might be done.

In phase 3, the counsellor concentrates on asking the client about the resourcing of what needs to be done. This is paralleled by the client's involvement in deciding to manage the problem so that an action plan may be devised and implemented. By way of a simple illustration, the phases that might be encapsulated in a client's thought process could run like this:

Phase	Client's thoughts	Task achieved
1	'I'm plateaued and finished'	defining
2	'I could get some training'	redefining
3	'I'll find out what's on offer'	managing

Signs that counselling is needed

The signs that might alert the general manager to the need for counselling are varied. They may possibly have physiological causes and be signs of illness. The intellectual ones are:

– muddled thinking
– lack of problem solving ability
– analysis paralysis
– tunnel vision
– inability to take a decision.

The physical ones are:

– lack of energy
– anxious appearance
– tense posture
– hyperactivity.

The behavioural ones are:

– ignoring others' feelings
– withdrawing socially
– changing management style abruptly
– becoming careless.

The emotional ones are:

– dullness of spirit
– lack of responsiveness to encouragement
– loss of achievement orientation.

These lists are only a guide and are by no means exhaustive. If these broad areas become too difficult for the general manager to handle, company policy and arrangements can be called into play. If none exist, then is the time for senior managers to exert some influence and make sure that there is a referral process. It must be in their interests to do so otherwise they will become involved with a problem that could potentially take up a lot of their time, energy and resources.

Adopting the counselling role

The ability to act as a counsellor requires that managers step out of their normal organizational role and into a counselling one. This involves making certain adjustments[8] on their part in order to deal with a subordinate's problems in a counselling mode. These can be contrasted as follows:

Managerial role	*Counselling role*
Company-centred	Client-centred
Evaluative	Non-evaluative
Accessible information	Confidential information
Power-oriented	Neutral
Staff receive problem	Staff own problem
Competitive listening	Collaborative listening
Argument justification	Client explanation

If some of these issues cannot be satisfactorily resolved, then it is in the best interests of all concerned, having opened up the dialogue, that the employee being counselled is seen in a more neutral situation. In some organizations, these dilemmas can be dealt with by reciprocal arrangements with other line managers to deal with the staff's difficulties. However, the possibility of conflict between personal and company interests can still arise. There may even be a point at which one of the managers' counsellors may, at a later date, assume some responsibility for a promotion. Once in possession of certain information gained in another context, it can be extremely difficult to discount it in decisions about, say, promotability, resilience or other required characteristic.

4.11 Conclusion

Successfully handling the challenges posed by managers' problems requires a combination of objectivity of decision and compassion in action. Managers do not find it easy to tell people that they are not performing satisfactorily, that they will not progress further in their careers or that they will be offered early retirement. This is so even though they believe it is the correct thing to do and want the problem urgently resolved.

These situations can be made easier if managers can, first of all, be made confident in their ability to handle them and, second, can offer some positive course of action. Alternatives, such as the ones suggested in this chapter, are a starting point and can have benefits for both the individual manager and the organization alike.

Action questions

SENIOR MANAGERS

Have you any problem managers? Are you able to spot them easily? What do you propose to do about them?

Do you feel confident in undertaking some first-line counselling with them?
Are you restricted in the range of options you can call into play to deal with them?

MANAGERS

If you had difficulties at work or at home that could affect your career, would you discuss them with your boss or human resources department?
Do you have any concerns about how you might be treated if *you* were in difficulties? What has happened in the past to others?

HUMAN RESOURCE SPECIALISTS

What procedures have you in place to deal with the career problems of managers?
How do they compare with 'best practice' elsewhere?
Are you able to fully support senior managers in obtaining solutions to career problems?

References

1. Davies, J., and Y. Deighan, 'The Managerial Menopause', *Personnel Management*, March 1986.
2. Hunt, J., and R. Collins, *Managers in Mid-Career Crisis*, Wellington Lane Press, 1983.
3. Gmelch, W., *Beyond Stress to Effective Management*, John Wiley, 1982.
4. Golzen, G., *Career Counselling for Senior Executives*, Kogan Page, 1988.
5. Institute of Personnel Management, *Personnel Management*, p. 17, April 1990.
6. Barry, A., 'A Phased Approach to Retirement Training', *Personnel Management*, February 1989.
7. Reddy, M., *The Manager's Guide to Counselling at Work*, BPS and Methuen, 1987.
8. Reddy, M., op. cit.

5
Career-linked
organizational
processes

5.1 Introduction

The way in which general managers can deal with the organizational challenges of facilitating (see Chapter 3) and handling problems of careers (see Chapter 4) is conditioned by the processes (dealt with in this chapter) and policies (see Chapter 6) operating in the organization. Going counter to the flow of these, deliberately or inadvertently, can cause problems for them or their staff. Understanding them and being able to recognize their impact on careers is fundamental to achieving harmony between individuals' personal and organizational goals and ensuring their satisfying and effective performance at work.

Surrounding these formal actions or routines are many informal, unwritten, unspoken aspects that are important to take into account if the codified procedures are to be effectively applied or negotiated in the organization. Dictionary meanings of the word 'process' vary: 'a series of actions that produce change or development; a method of doing or producing or doing something; a forward movement'. The use of the word process here is intended to encapsulate all of these aspects. Two key processes that are intertwined throughout an organizational career are the impact the organization has on the individual, for example, as in socialization, mentioned in Chapter 3, and the effect the individual has on the organization in terms of new ideas values and techniques.

Many factors can have a powerful effect on careers, either before or at the moment of entry into the organization, whether this be the image presented at recruitment or the manager labelling the new employee as having potential. These modify and shape the managers' career aspirations and chances of fulfilling them before they even start work.

One company, unbeknown to its recruits, who were all judged to be competent graduates, further subdivided them into alphas, betas and gammas. Alphas were clear certainties for top management level, betas were probables and gammas possible but unlikely. This categorization conditioned how senior management viewed them and the assignments allocated to them. It also determined the kind of grading and pay curve they would follow and their respective time scales for promotion.

Other processes, such as appraisal, assessment and the use of development centres, serve on a continuous basis to steer or reinforce organizational career directions. If applied by senior management with sensitivity and involvement, these can be a powerful tool for positive career development and change.

The areas relating to organizational processes covered in this chapter are:

– recruiting for current job competences
– recruiting for potential job competences
– selection in whose image?
– induction
– corporate cultural influences on careers
– internal career networks
– links to external career networks
– appraisal systems
– assessment centres
– development centres.

5.2 Recruiting for current job competences

Most recruitment is to fulfil a specific, current organizational need for work performance rather than for some time in the future. The latter kind of thinking is usually associated with the recruitment and training of graduates who, for the most part, have no directly applicable experience and training to offer and are thus employed for their potential performance.

Managerial competences

At the time of writing, much interest is being generated by the term managerial competences in relation to job performance. It is worth outlining this debate as the lists of competences that organizations draw up for themselves affect the whole process of career development within these organizations. Recruitment, induction, training appraisal, promotion, remuneration, counselling and cultural context are all areas that may be modified by them.

ARRIVING AT A LIST OF COMPETENCES

First, definitions vary according to whose research or organizational base is used. The layman may use 'competence' to mean the ability to perform some specific job. Other definitions relate not just to adequate performance but to a superior one. Still others define a competence as an ability, skill or personality trait or, more generally, as a willingness and ability to perform a task.

Second, there is the question of usage. Abilities, knowledge, skills and attitudes and personality may contribute to the possession of a competence, but its *use* depends on the *context*. For example, the performance and measurement of the competence of being able to swim looks very different in the open sea compared to in a swimming pool, with ordinary clothes rather than a swimming costume and whether one is escaping from a sinking ship or diving from the pool-side.

Third, there is a debate about the numbers of competences and how they are arrived at. As many as 40 competences have appeared in lists in the published literature. These are then usually regrouped into four or five main clusters , such as interpersonal, intellectual and so on.

Competences are arrived at by a variety of methods and statistical analysis, which may explain, in part, the variation in their numbers and grouping. The first source of ideas may be a panel of senior managers assessing what they think is important to successful job performance and they may themselves be observed and studied to determine the difference between adequate and outstanding performance. A series of 'critical incidents' in managerial work may also be elicited and analysed for clues. The next stage is to see how these differentiating characteristics can be measured.

Competences such as creativity, flexibility, tolerance of ambiguity and coping with change are harder to define and assess and require a number of different approaches. There is also the thorny problem of whether competences for successful managers are universal or organization-specific. Then there is the question of how they are related to each other and whether there are syndromes of behaviour, such as those associated with introversion or extraversion. Last, it may be asked when putting competences to work whether the absence of one can be compensated for by the presence of another. On the subject of recruitment and selection, there is the issue of squaring these procedures with equal opportunities policies if certain competences are more likely to be found in some social, educational and ethnic groupings rather than in others.

RESULTS OF INSTITUTING THIS SYSTEM

The thinking about corporate culture and the various comparative studies on successful organizations in the same sector would suggest that a substantial number of competences are organization-specific (a contingency model) rather than universal. The fact that BP, Cadbury-Schweppes, NatWest, BAT and Shell are all working on their own particular versions suggests that they want something to reflect their own strategy, structure and culture rather than relying on a general view of what a good manager is and does. That said, it is possible to find some similarities in the content of the competences, although the labels may be different.

The point here is that recruitment for current competences will reinforce both the weaknesses as well as the strengths of the organization. This is because the outcome of the recruitment process will ensure continuity and conformity. If those who have risen in a risk-aversed culture believe that the difference in outstanding and adequate performance is rarely making mistakes, then that will be considered at recruitment, later rewarded and so the culture will be perpetuated. On the other hand, if it is desirable that an entrepreneurial competence be encouraged, then a significant number of those with that competence will need to be recruited. This would ensure that a critical number of staff possessing this quality are present to overcome the stereotypes of the assessing managers, otherwise the competence will disappear through extinction or wastage.

5.3 Recruiting for potential job competences

Difficulties

Where the interest is in recruitment for *future* competences, decisions and methodologies become more difficult. Accurate prediction of what organizations need becomes more problematical and any predictive assessment methodology is, by its very nature, likely to contain more errors. There will probably always be a requirement for competences like 'adaptability to change' or 'capacity to learn', but other, more specific, competences will change. BP, who have researched extensively in the competence field, advise that any competence model needs to be checked about every two years to ensure that it continues to reflect the company's needs.

Another difficulty in recruiting young managers for potential competence is that the very presence of certain desirable attributes for future roles, such as creativity or innovation, may not make it easy for them to conform to their present job requirements. Waiting for the chance to use them in their senior appointment to come can be particularly frustrating and may cause them to leave. They may be seen as difficult to manage, reluctant to be corporate citizens and, thus, not proceed in a predictable way with the main task required of them. The other possibility is that those very competences may be directly extinguished by a strong company culture or simply atrophy through lack of use.

Ways of dealing with these

The optimist camp would argue strongly that management has to identify strengths and build on talent that cannot be implanted easily. Therefore, recruiting for future talent is imperative and the organization should alter its practices to ensure that this occurs.

One senior manager argued that if certain valuable competences have been identified in an individual early on and would be valued in three to five years' time, then the organization should be capable of finding a suitable opening. While the manager could easily see the possibility of this being done for a few people, it was accepted that this could be a problem if those with potential were more actively recruited, thus raising the numbers of those whose careers needed to be developed.

5.4 Selection in whose image?

Even if the recruitment procedures are working well to attract people with the right competences, those doing the initial screening and making the final decisions are in a very powerful position. CEOs can influence many of the informal as well as the formal criteria that operate during the recruitment and promotion processes. One view[1] is that these filter down and become embodied in the organization's thinking.

A key dimension here is the degree of diversity, as opposed to the amount of homogeneity, desired within a particular company. This is seen in several ways.

Some functions dominate or are thought to be more prestigious in organizations, even when they are in similar businesses. For example, in Westinghouse it has been qualifications in engineering that have been important for one's career, while in General Electric it has been qualifications in marketing and finance. Where appropriate, the CEO can help to change this by ensuring that other functions are represented at more senior positions and on the board.

Second, some selection decisions may be unduly influenced by where managers were educated and in which organizational 'stables' they trained. Particular interests thought to be valuable in doing business (golf or sailing) and appearance for the client base (such as in the City) can also be informal criteria.

Third, the amount of parochialism that exists in the firm can, through excessive loyalty, divert energy from the corporate direction, especially when mobility of staff is needed. This is because managers in different units will want to retain able people or decision makers and staff may feel committed and not wish to poach or be poached. One way of reducing this is through a company-wide career development scheme. A senior manager knows that the loss of someone trained will be compensated for by the fact that other senior manages will also have to release an able manager for the 'corporate good'.

A recent study of 450 CEOs analysed on 59 variables[2] compared them to others in the top management team. They possessed certain common attributes that generated over time an image and ability to be self-reliant. Their childhood tended to be more cosmopolitan. Early management experience was multifunctional and international, and their middle management career was profit centre oriented. As a CEO their style was interventionist and directive. The results of the survey were said to

certainly indicate that current British CEOs would replicate their own experience.

This could imply that they are reinforcing a cadre of corporate clones who may not be appropriate in the future. Self-reliance and a directive management style, compared to team play and supportive management behaviour, run counter to predictions of the required future styles in organizations. It is also widely recognized by selectors and assessors themselves that they need to be on their guard against employing clones. This is why thorough training in interviewing and assessment techniques is recommended before embarking on recruitment and promotion exercises. The general manager can play a crucial part here in making selection more objective by becoming actively involved in the specification process of the type of manager wanted and being part of the selection team.

5.5 Induction

Once recruited, a manager has to settle in. This process has been covered from an individual perspective in Chapter 3 in the sections on career transitions and the socialization of managers. From an organizational viewpoint, there are other aspects that need to be considered, such as the nature of the induction itself and the forms it can take.

Early induction and/or training are processes that give the new recruit information and instil values about the organization. It is a time of attempts to influence the manager by senior and other managers and a trial at moulding the newcomer into the ways of the corporate culture through direct and more subtle forms of communication. Therefore, induction can be thought of as a three-part communication chain[3] where a breakdown in one area will affect the success of the induction as a whole:

- *source*: credibility, trustworthiness, power and status, consistency with other messages from the same or other sources
- *message*: accuracy, realism, importance, frequency specificity, positive or negative, quantity of information, one- or two-way
- *receiver*: preconceptions, past experiences, self-confidence and so on.

Each part also has certain characteristics that have to be carefully communicated. An information source that is not credible will not successfully convey a message, however positive.

Communication

The communication process, that is, the content and the manner in which it is communicated, is important for 'critical period learning' to take place. Certain language and skills need to be acquired and tests of initiation may be undergone before colleagueship is accepted. For instance, when Joan entered the marketing department of a firm making consumer products, the first job she was given was to devise a marketing and sales information system that would ensure that the data gleaned from the field sales force about their clients' business (average stock levels for particular items, business plans, outlets and so on) could be turned into customer business profiles. This would then be used to fine tune the implementation of the marketing strategy through the setting of sales targets, customer support and promotional material.

On starting to gather information about the project, Joan was frequently put off by the message, 'We've tried that 4 times in the last 10 years and it's never got off the ground – why should you succeed?' Joan eventually *did* succeed by working as part of a team with the sales managers, covering three main product areas. The sales force was reassured that the information they produced would not reduce the value of their unique contribution of knowing the customer, which as salesmen they jealously guarded. Instead, their appraisal listed it as an important activity and upon which special performance payments were made. However, this exercise had always been given to newcomers who did not know about the accumulated cynicism. The divisional director had used this test as a means of getting newcomers to know the culture and workings of the department in the hope that they would succeed in solving the problem.

Forms of induction

COOK'S TOURS AND WORK SHADOWING

The forms that induction can take are several. 'Cook's tours', spending a relatively short time in a department or job, say one to six months, and work shadowing, following a senior person to learn job, are two possibilities.

These have frequently been used for graduates or junior management jobs but have their drawbacks as there is lack of real commitment for both parties. They are also less suitable for middle or more senior managers who want to take charge of a job. However, IBM use the personal assistant method of growing some of their high-flyers by giving them a taste of the level and pace of work associated with senior management positions. Similarly, secretaries to ministers in the Civil Service are senior managers who already have administrative and drafting skills but who need to acquire an overview of a department.

Other organizations are insistent on exposing all new recruits, including middle and senior management to their core business. For example, British Airways makes them spend time at Heathrow Airport, London, talking with passengers as they come off aeroplanes. Topics covered are facilities, comfort or whatever aspects the managers see as relevant to their specialism, such as medical, information technology and so on. Such live, early experiences can make a lasting impression on the new recruit.

WORKING IN PAIRS OR TEAMS

In the professions, induction may take this form so that the newcomer is shown the boundaries of behaviour when dealing with clients and the way to deal with crises and mistakes. Alternatively, senior managers may be given an office in their new organization a few months in advance of their appointment. This can be a most productive time for the manager to talk informally to colleagues and sense the mood, forces for and against change and the likely alliances and political groupings that exist.

FORMAL AND INFORMAL

Professionals may find a formal induction process harder to accept since they bring to the organization an additional set of values (such as technical competence and freedom) introduced early in their training. In the aerospace division of a major engineering company, professional expertise was such a strong value that specialists would not publicly disagree with one another. If anyone was said to have a view on some matter, it meant that they were violently opposed to it. The recruit would be sensitized to this as early as possible by colleagues.

An informal test of whether the induction is complete is to know what rules exist but which are not written down. For example, some partnerships persist in signing memos with initials, even when there may be 400 individuals and 15 times that number of people in the organization. The scope for error is considerable internally, as names and initials of junior staff can be the same as those of partners. This causes enormous confusion to the switchboard and clients. Similarly, alphabetical listings of professional and support staff give no idea where a working relationship exists between junior and senior staff. Knowledge of these practices are expected to be acquired informally and their mastery indicates provisional membership of the 'club'.

5.6 Corporate cultural influences on careers

During the induction process, the new recruit begins to have an idea of what constitutes career success in the organization's terms, the facilitators and constraints surrounding it and who the kingmakers and patrons are. There may be norms regarding timetables for promotion, tolerance of failure and ease of crossing functional boundaries.

Timetables

Timetables can be very important regulators of career progress within organizations and being ahead or behind them can be a source of anxiety and frustration. Consultancy, for example, is traditionally known as a young person's career, with promotion to director in large firms occurring between 35 and 40 years of age. Similarly, in legal and accountancy practices, partnerships are offered between 32 and 35 years. In small, fast-growing computer firms, the managing director could be 30 years old. In contrast, heads of functions in large bureaucratic organizations may not reach that position until they are 40 years old or older.

Performance within these unwritten age bands is eagerly watched by individuals and their peers alike. Nominations for particular development programmes may thus be a significant milestone, signalling potential success and being true to form in the promotability stakes.

Risk taking

Tolerance of failure varies widely within and between sectors and organizations. Clearing banks have traditionally had a risk-aversed culture (for example, in the approval of loans) and senior positions went to those who conformed with this behaviour. Now, with opportunities arising for new products and services and financial management advice, these attitudes are not as highly valued as they once were as entrepreneurial and specialist skills are called for.

In contrast with this attitude, other organizations will take the view that anyone who is not making any mistakes is not being stretched and therefore is not learning. A director of a London-based public relations firm maintains that after an unsuccessful bid for an account, the team will all sit together and analyse what went wrong and what could have been done better. This process is always started by the director herself. It is intended to demonstrate that the philosophy 'I did not get where I am today by never making mistakes' is acceptable.

Other cultures breed a climate of always needing to appear successful, as peer influences can be important in channelling work, obtaining new clients or reviewing performance. However, the learning that does occur here is bound to be limited, apart from that involved in always maintaining appearances.

Boundaries

The ease with which organizational and functional boundaries can be crossed is another factor that governs career success through providing multiple routes and general management experience. The degree of ease is the expression of values involving openness, lack of the need to protect empires, the transcendence of corporate needs over local ones and an interest in cross-fertilization of ideas.

It is not uncommon in organizations to find quite senior people who are threatened by those who show an inclination and ability to cross organizational or disciplinary boundaries. This may be so even where the value of being able to operate in this way is overtly encouraged and even endorsed by the board.

Mobility

Organizations that value mobility encourage frequent movement between jobs as a means of career development. After as little as two years, there is the expectation of a transfer being proposed and alarm may be experienced if this has not occurred by year three.

The reverse situation can also apply. The author recalls an interview with a senior buyer in a public sector organization who answered a question on business policy thus: I don't know; I've only been here 6 years. You had better ask a colleague who has been here 30 years.

Cultures

Whether an organization encourages internal career mobility or not may depend on the type of help likely to be available[4] in a particular culture:[5]

- *power cultures*, which rely on one key person at the centre who controls the organization, would tend to discourage helping as the view would be that people should stand on their own merits and develop their own careers
- *role cultures*, where jobs have to fit the mission and systems in the organization, value the precision gained by instructing and might discourage experimentation as a valid means of learning and enhancing one's career
- *task cultures*, which are teams centred around problem solving and arranged in a matrix of project and function, attach importance to coaching as a means of progressing careers
- *person cultures*, organizations that serve the purposes of their star performers, may be more receptive to monitoring.

These four cultures have wider implications for careers in general. In the power culture, which are usually small, entrepreneurial companies in property or finance, career success depends on being an extension of the boss and being valued by members of the 'inner circle'. In a role culture, such as the civil and public service, the oil or automobile industries, the existence of several hierarchical layers means that individuals can be promoted but stay in the same functional specialism. They may well be over 45 before they are able to gain general management experience. With task cultures, whose structures are variable, such as in project engineering companies, consultancies and computer software firms, ones' boss also keeps changing and there may be no established career route. The ambiguity of having two bosses at the same time (functional and project) thus makes a difficult situation worse. Finally, the person culture, seen in small consultancies, barristers' chambers and architects' practices, is unlikely to have a career structure at all. This is because the organization primarily serves the needs of the individuals rather than the other way round. Individuals create their own career and the onus is on them for self-development and advancement, with a mentor if they are lucky.

A person's career will also depend on the extent to which they can wholeheartedly embrace the values of the culture in which they find themselves. Pollution, wastage of natural resources, concern for employees and the type of work the organization does will all affect career prospects. For example, some individuals will refuse to work for a tobacco company or organizations involved in nuclear or defence research.

One example is Bill, a 37-year-old married man with three children who had trained as an industrial engineer. He found himself plateaued in a divisional management services department. He was offered a promotion in another subsidiary manufacturing defence systems (not arms). He turned it down on moral grounds. The company then searched the group for a position of a comparable grade but without success. He left the company without a job to take up, causing considerable anxiety to all his family who nevertheless backed him in his decision.

Examining the company culture can also help to explain why some competent and socially skilled individuals are a success in one organization and not in another. One classification of culture[6] that is useful here is based on the degree of risk and speed of feedback in the work of the organization.

The 'macho' culture tends to be found in organizations concerned with advertising, venture capital, property development and broking. The risks are high and the feedback is fast in these sorts of businesses as the situation can change overnight. What is valued is flair, individualism, competitiveness and resilience. Successful careers are built on the possession and appropriate use of these abilities.

In contrast, the 'work hard/play hard' culture is found in organizations that deal with the sales of mass consumer goods and in the retail sector. The risks are relatively low in that no single sale will make or break the organization and the feedback from the market is fast (say, the analysis of weekly sales figures). The expressed values are that the company is sales driven, success comes through persistence and team effort and groups compete against each other for the best results.

The 'process culture', by contrast, is the bureaucratic organization – retail banks, insurance and public utilities falling into this group. Risks are widely shared and the feedback is slow. The organizational values are order, accuracy, sharing of decision making responsibility, multiple documentation and backup copies to provide cover for one's own part in business procedures.

The last type is 'bet your company'. Here the organizational activity is likely to be in capital goods manufacture, heavy equipment, oil and investment banks. Risks are high (as in oil exploration) and feedback is slow, hence the emphasis is on central planning and control. The values espoused are cautious decision making, maturity and experience.

It is easy to see, therefore, how organizations, by a process of survival of the fittest, encourage certain types of career behaviour. Patterns may become so ingrained as to make it difficult for long-serving individuals to alter their values and behaviour and successfully transfer out of the system. Indeed, were they to do so, they might feel very uncomfortable as their expectations of what is right may not be shared by other organizations.

A culture can so reinforce the pattern of what is judged as career success that it becomes detrimental to the survival of the organization if a change in strategic direction is required. For example, one very large retail organization was, for historical reasons, buyer-led. The senior positions were occupied, in the main, by buyers or by those closely associated with that function. The result was that marketing and market research were virtually non-existent as functions. Where information did surface, it was always forced to take second place to what the buyers 'really knew about the market'. The organization was thus deprived of vital strategic information. It could not retain its able people at middle management levels as they saw little prospect of advancement if they were not from the buying function. When, eventually, group results were so poor that they could no longer be ignored, an outside review was commissioned. These anomalies were subsequently rectified, enabling a more balanced structure and a way forward in the progressing of careers.

Furthermore, it must be mentioned that the values placed on certain functions can be critical in determining the career ceiling. For example, the management of functions within firms of professionals is often seen to be of less importance than the work of the professionals themselves. Functional heads usually report to an administration or other partner to ensure that the pervading professional culture is always brought to bear on any new functional values that may be introduced. Until advertising restrictions were recently lifted, active marketing of the professions was seen as challenging the discreet, personal process of work being referred by word of mouth. Consequently, it took a while before marketing specialists were regarded as professionals in their own right, with their own values, requirements and professional bodies. Similarly, in some large bureaucracies and in the Civil Service, the belief in the supremacy of the generalist still survives. The power of the expert specialists is always curbed by a limit on the top grades to which they may aspire and by their having always to report to a generalist. Senior managers may therefore need to ensure that the performance requirements and career success of their staff are compatible with and enhanced by the corporate culture. If they value particular managers' contributions, they may have to prevent them being swamped by the cultural imperatives acting on career.

5.7 Internal career networks

Internal career networks form part of the company culture and help to sustain its pervasive influence. Many of these networks arise from the recruitment, selection and induction processes mentioned earlier in this chapter. For example, some companies use a cohort approach to their graduate intake. This can later provide an opportunity for mutual support and information in seeking out opportunities. Sometimes 'pacts' may be made to reinforce each others' reputations whenever possible.

Fast-streamers, unlike an age cohort, assume the mantle of the élite and also act in a supportive and respectful manner to each other (if they are not in direct competition). Those who were passed by a particular panellist or line manager may believe that they have something in common, such as toughness.

A third type of career network can arise from being part of the international circuit group. This can provide a powerful communications network and resource group among senior managers as mere membership is enough to command mutual respect.

Membership of these last two groups, however, can put a ceiling on the prospects of others. This applies especially to the international circuit where key jobs will always be offered first to the chosen few and is particularly evident in multinationals where 'home' nationals have tended to predominate in many of the senior positions as they are felt to embody both the corporate and the home culture.

Alliances may also spring up based on functional or locational groupings. This can be a form of solidarity when numbers are small. For example, divisional IT or marketing researchers may be the lone professional and may feel unduly exposed when offering advice or taking decisions. Contacts with similar specialists elsewhere in the organization help to reduce this feeling of isolation and may provide advance notice of career opportunities.

Second, career stables (locations that have produced 'good people' over a long period of time) tend to perpetuate themselves. They are seen in the organization as useful places to pass through, not only for experience but for automatic 'club' membership. The web of contacts then permeates the whole organization and carries its influence up to board level.

Last, but not least, is the membership of particular committees or task forces that, if successful, confer a mutual belief of superiority.

Networks are therefore ways of helping or hindering managers' effectiveness and of enhancing or diminishing their reputations. That is why they are so crucial in determining career success. Senior managers will be well aware of these networks and who the key players are. They are therefore able to facilitate contacts at an appropriate level for their own staff.

5.8 Links to external career networks

External career networks are included in this chapter as they can have an influence on the use made of internal networks and on a managers' career aspirations. Moreover, some roles and functions within organizations are more amenable than others to participating in these external networks. Public relations, human resources management, information management and finance are some of the areas where managers will have an eye on the external context of their jobs. All this is also a useful reminder to organizations that there are aspects of their managers' careers that they cannot control unless they volunteer information about them. The importance of these external networks to careers is seen in the use made of them when individuals wish to move from organizations or to develop new business.

University alumni and MBA networks are now widespread, with handbooks and events to sustain the membership and encourage consultation. Similar processes exist for those who have been on non-examinable management courses.

The vast array of trade associations and professional bodies also exert a powerful influence on careers and in some cases this overrides the pull of the employing organization. Cultivating a high external profile is often the way individuals make themselves approachable to other organizations. A relevant activity here is speaking at conferences and being involved in local community work, especially subcommittees of local councils, which may be a corridor for new career openings.

All these activities start to raise the profile of individuals to the point that they are recommended by others to headhunters. Once on the circuit, a new wave of opportunities opens up. The approach, typically, is to ask whether you know of anyone who might be interested (including oneself) and never to divulge the source of one's name.

Headhunting is a highly competitive business and the reputable companies do not approach an individual they have placed with a client for an agreed period of time. Nor would they poach from within their client list, thus inviting withdrawal of business. They vary in their methods from interviews through to whole batteries of tests and procedures, but personal introductions are the bedrock of their activities.

Some senior executives are happy to be approached by them as a means of staying in touch with their marketability and assessing their career prospects. Indeed, they are a form of external appraisal. They indicate the degree of transferability of an individual's career experience and as such are a barometer that the general manager needs to watch.

5.9 Appraisal systems

Along with the many networks that an individual might use, the appraisal system is a key launch pad in the organizational career. Although the forms and frequency of appraisal and the seriousness with which it is taken can vary widely, some generalizations can be made.

It is used in several ways that affect career planning and development. Administratively, it can provide a felt-fair way of deciding on promotions and transfers and, in some cases, remuneration, although current thinking is that appraisal and compensation should be separate. They also provide the organization as a whole with a means of acquiring information about the level and type of skills available, the likely surplus and deficits of skilled manpower in the future and the requirements for succession planning (see Chapter 2). An aggregate of assessments of promotability and training needs allow a centralized assessment of the rate at which business strategy and change can be achieved with the existing resources within the organization. It provides the employee with a strong motivation for self-development, too, with the regular setting of tasks and the analysis of personal strengths and weaknesses.

The success of appraisal in general, but in particular as a basis for career decision making, depends on the level of trust that managers can elicit from their staff and the ability of both to set clear, achievable objectives.

From the viewpoint of the appraiser, an appraisal helps to facilitate the personal career goals of the employee. It also creates an awareness of strengths and weaknesses that can be used as a basis for coaching to reach the mutual goals of the appraisee and appraiser. At the same time, the potential problems can be dealt with early on. This prevents them from becoming serious and perhaps spoiling two careers for the lack of a planned, formal discussion. Increased staff performance and commitment should follow, which in turn will enhance the employees' career prospects.

Through appraisal, the person being appraised is given a better chance to exert control over his or her career direction by making known the hopes, aspirations and any constraints that might affect their attainment. In particular, having a part in the setting of goals and the conditions under which they can be achieved ensures that they are owned. The senior manager or appraiser can then facilitate their achievement by helping to remove any likely disrupting factors under his or her control. The mere regularity of an appraisal ensures the continual reassessment of the questions:

- 'What am I doing?'
- 'Do I enjoy doing it?'
- 'Am I still learning?'
- 'Is it preparing me for something else?'

A good review from the appraised's viewpoint will emphasize the future in terms of growth and development and an action plan to which both parties will contribute. The general manager can support the manager by checking out the action plan to which both parties will contribute. Furthermore the process can be facilitated by seeing that the action plan is being carried out and by helping to remove any organizational constraints. Where both parties agree that there are areas of doubt, a lack of information can readily be tested through the use of, say, assessment centres.

5.10 Assessment centres

In addition to recruitment and selection for current vacancies, many organizations are now using assessment centres as a means of sharpening up appraisal decisions on promotability and individual potential. They can also be used as an organization development planning tool to see what the pool of available talent is like across the organization and therefore form the basis of succession planning. Another related but special use in career planning is that of development centres (which is covered in the next section).

Assessment centres are tools for improving managerial decision making in the human resources field and are based on systematic, analytical and observational procedures. They are more reliable than interviews alone and utilize a number of different techniques to improve accuracy and reliability. The design procedure is critical to their utility and success and starts with a job analysis. This taps many sources of data with different techniques such as the repertory grid (a tool to extract dimensions on which people make judgements), observation, structured interviews and so on. In the case of selection decisions, the dimensions related to successful job performance will be based on current criteria. Where the assessment of potential is concerned, estimates have to be made in the light of strategy documents, possible changes in structure and skill levels required, as well as knowing what these latent skills and attributes might look like in current job holders. Once these are known, the task is to find suitable measures that can be elicited and observed, so that at least two trained assessors can agree on the evidence. This does not mean that differences are ignored. On the contrary, if they exist, discussion continues until the reasons can be exposed. The outcome is usually a much more subtle judgement about the candidate, who may well display contradictory behaviour during the assessment.

Assessment centres have to be tailored but a 'composite' might be something like this. Candidates arrive in the evening in time for dinner to enable them to relax and get to know other participants and staff before the two-day programme starts. While this part of the process is not formally evaluated, observations and incidents do not pass unnoticed. Sometimes behaviour in this setting will contrast with that shown in certain exercises and provide a stimulus to further probing. A group may contain up to 12 participants and these can be subdivided for group exercises into fours or sixes to allow 'air time' for individuals. The day is a combination of techniques that are often only used individually in selection procedures because of time constraints:

- in-tray exercises
- job samples – realistic problems, for example, customer care, consultancy or a management dilemma or a report
- role playing
- group discussion
- psychometric tests of aptitude, ability, interest and personality
- group tasks
- individual problem solving
- case studies
- presentations.

As a whole, these should enable participants to show the behaviours and traits that the assessors believe are related to successful job performance now or in the future. There is no one correct formula, but stimulation, variety and interest will be the motivating factors for all involved.

Managing the assessment and assessors

The time allocations and overall pace are also important. If participants are kept waiting, the momentum is lost. Conversely, too much hustling drives performance to the mediocre, encouraging solutions where issues are not explored or consensus is achieved by vote rather than persuasion or argument. It should also be remembered that assessment centres are very powerful ways of communicating an organization's image and culture. The assessors and administrative staff are themselves being assessed. Wrong instructions, incomplete handouts, poor timekeeping and confusion over room allocations have a disproportionate effect in these circumstances as everything else is being carefully graded.

Managing the assessors (committed, senior managers who understand the process) is itself an important function so that all exercises, panel reviews and discussions are completed to time. A chairman of assessors, which may include a human resources specialist, is usually appointed so that all data can be collated systematically, overall rankings of participants can be made and feedback carefully prepared.

In difficult cases, the assessing team will all discuss the problems so that the final feedback-giver is well briefed. Rejected candidates may go away with the impression of having failed if they are not selected, even if they find out that they dislike the organization and/or the appraisers. The fact that this is public may make matters worse. Feedback needs to be constructive. The observation that someone is cautious, reflective, thoughtful and analytical may be a disadvantage in the sales force of a fast-moving consumer goods organization, but an advantage in the planning department of an oil company. Therefore, the results have to be used in a balanced way.

Dilemmas

Assessment centres have their own associated dilemmas. For example, in the cases discussed, the organization keeps the detailed information if the centre has been used for external assessment. If it is internal, the human resources department, line managers and assessors all have access to it. For how long will these records be kept? Some organizations specify a cut-off period while others do not. Will reference be made to them regarding future postings?

A second problem is the degree to which the centres are tailored to the individual organization – which involves proper investment of time, effort and support – to individual divisions or functions, or to families of jobs? The more specific, the less likelihood there is of there being a range of candidates who will stimulate interaction and so it will be used less often. However, they will be more likely to pick up the subtle factors that differentiate successful performance rather than expecting 'common core' factors to apply across a large group. Furthermore, in-company materials will appear more credible but carry the risk of people trying to apply directly their old experience. Third, the establishment of criteria (success dimensions) is a difficult enough task on its own. However, decisions still have to be made (even if criteria have been pre-weighted) as to how they will be combined and if meeting some of them very adequately compensates for the absence of or weaknesses in others.

Validation

Validation is a vital part of the whole exercise. No one can expect that the process will be right the first time, which is why some follow-up is necessary. This enables the designers to see what proportion of the decisions held good in relation to job performance, which exercises gave the most useful measurements and how these related to the overall scores on ratings achieved. While senior managers may think that such a process is tedious, time-consuming and involves extra cost, the whole credibility of the method (and therefore line management support) will be at stake. Line managers will not offer themselves as potential assessors, willing to be trained for two days or more, if they have a fear of being linked with a possible failure in organizational procedures.

Benefits

The main benefits associated with this method are, first, better quality decision making than that based on interviews alone. As one manager said, 'the centre stopped at least one candidate who would have passed the interview procedure'.

Second, the assessing panel has the benefit of being able to compare candidates simultaneously on similar tasks rather than trying to remember individuals from weeks back.

Third, it speeds up decision making as all assessors are forced to take a view. They are under peer pressure and the team has to give a specific answer and feedback to the waiting participants.

The cost

Costs are not readily forthcoming from organizations, but it should be relatively easy to cost the managers' time in days, the use of an external consultant if necessary to help in the design, production of and training in the use of specific materials.

A helpful exercise in all this is to calculate the cost of a poor decision. This puts the overall investment in the assessment centre approach into perspective.

A good way in which general managers can extract the maximum benefit from assessment centres is to make sure that they are consulted and involved at every stage. Most importantly, they should ask for some validation study to be carried out.

5.11 Development centres

Development centres use similar techniques to those of assessment centres, but there are some important differences. The objectives are to identify precise, individual development needs. This is sometimes to meet future management requirements, such as has been done within BT, or, in other cases, for example DEC, to encourage self-development. The difference is illustrated[7] in the following situation.

A person might receive a low overall rating on, say, analytical ability that is then used to reject that person for a particular job or promotion. In a development centre, that information is used to create a performance improvement plan through a counselling procedure. The feedback in BT's case is given primarily for the benefit of the participant, although the line manager may want an overall account. Their approach has been to give limited feedback about their main strengths and development needs, often with the participant present. DEC, on the other hand, give all the results back to the participants. It is up to them to decide how they will approach this and many, if not most, will enlist the help of their line manager.

The long-term benefit of this approach is that it encourages individuals to tackle something manageable and at their own pace. When they do eventually apply for a promotion, they know what to expect and may have remedied deficiencies that would previously have ruled them out straight away. This approach is more difficult to sell internally as the benefits are longer term and more diffuse.

The investment in development centres will be more readily accepted if the organization believes itself to be a learning community. The results can then also be linked to career planning and succession planning as participants come away with a more realistic assessment of themselves and their aspirations, as is said to happen within IBM. However, there is always the risk that this may lead to the mutual conclusion that there is no future career left, if personal and organizational needs do not coincide. Alternatively, some adherents to this approach say that commitment to the organization increases.

In general, development centres have been successfully implemented when the organization is labour intensive or has a large number of difficult-to-replace professionals. Investment in them may then be seen as a motivator, resulting in increased longer-term retention of staff.

5.12 Conclusion

Being aware of the organizational processes that affect career means that general managers are more likely to enable the successful career planning and management of the staff working for them. They may also have the chance to identify where some of these processes have a negative effect on the careers of their otherwise able and motivated staff. By using their influence to remove them, they may increase commitment and retention, which can only be to the good of their own operating unit's performance and, ultimately, their own careers.

Action questions

SENIOR MANAGERS

Are you influencing the organizational processes that affect the careers of your managers?
Are you helping your managers to read the informal aspects of the organization that affect their careers?

MANAGERS

Do you know what the appropriate models of career success are in the organization?
Are you aware of the various networks to which you might belong and how they might help you in your career?
Do you feel as if you are a participant in the organization or more of a detached observer? Do you belong?

HUMAN RESOURCE SPECIALISTS

Are the organizational processes for which you are responsible seen to be helpful in career planning and management or are they merely complied with?
Do you need to involve senior managers more closely with their design, execution and evaluation?

References

1. Sayles, L., and R. Wright, 'The Use of Culture in Strategic Management', *Issues and Observations*, Vol. 5, No. 4, Centre for Creative Leadership, 1988.
2. Norburn, D., 'The Chief Executive: A breed apart', *Strategic Management Journal*, Vol. 10, June 1988.

3. Jablin, F., and N. Jablin, 'Organizational Entry, Assimilation and Exit', in F. Jablin, L. Putnam, K. Roberts, *Handbook of Organizational Communication*, Sage, 1987.
4. Megginson, D., 'Instructor, Coach, Mentor: Three ways of helping for managers', *Management Education and Development*, Vol. 19, 1988.
5. Harrison, R., 'How to Describe Your Organization', *Harvard Business Review*, September/October 1972.
6. Deal, T., and A. Kennedy, *Corporate Cultures: The rites and rituals of corporate life*, Addison Wesley, 1982.
7. Rodger, D., and C. Maybey, 'BT's Leap Forward From Assessment Centres', *Personnel Management*, July 1987.

6
Career-linked
organizational policies

6.1 Introduction

Implications of current trends

Corporate policies relating directly or indirectly to careers are beginning
to be questioned by those whom they affect. The increasing demands by
staff for more flexibility in how and where they wish to work, the growing
numbers of dual career couples and the rapidly increasing opportunities
for self-development are undermining the automatic conformance to
corporate systems of employment. Moreover, one cannot assume that
everyone is aiming for promotion, is willing to be a mobile high-flyer and
is prepared to leave behind their specialist or professional training. At the
same time, this relatively new-found freedom to shape one's own career
can bring its own dilemmas and stresses because there is less predictability
and security. Furthermore, individuals have to take more responsibility
for their decisions (rather than taking any frustration out on the organization) if things go wrong.

General managers operating in a more autonomous way because of
structural changes in their organizations will therefore need to assess
whether these corporate policies are working for or against them. Where
necessary, they may need to adapt or dispense with them. They will need
to run a flexible and responsive organization without creating perceived
disparity of treatment among their managers. This task will be made easier
if their organization can offer a broad range of options in employment and
career development. In trying to achieve this new approach, senior
managers will be faced with decisions that could break new ground in
policy making. They will undoubtedly accumulate a rich source of experience in dealing with individual needs and could contribute greatly to the
development and monitoring of career-linked organizational policies. For
simplicity, these policies have been grouped under two broad headings
according to their prime focus:

- *organizational*:
  - late entrants and recruitment stereotypes
  - high-flyers and flyers
  - generalists or multispecialists?
  - specialists into line managers?
  - promotion
  - compensation and benefits
  - corporate development programmes
- *individual*:
  - open learning facilities
  - sponsoring individual qualifications
  - open learning
  - career break schemes
  - child and family care provision
  - workplace counselling

These policies do not operate in isolation from each other or from the career challenges and the problems and processes described in Chapters 3, 4 and 5 respectively. Indeed, they will affect how they can be dealt with in a way that allows the organization to find an acceptable balance between individual needs and corporate requirements.

6.2 Late entrants and recruitment stereotypes

The widely publicized general and specific skills shortages mentioned in Chapter 2 means that some organizations are critically reviewing their policies and practices relating to the recruitment of the older worker. The 'too old at 40' stereotype is having to be revised (along with some of the others). It was often used as a simple screening device for recruiters inundated with applications generated by advertising in national newspapers or professional journals. Even now, search consultants are reluctant to go against their clients' instructions on this matter.

Is there a basis in fact for these stereotypes?

The stereotypes that persist seem difficult to believe in view of the age of heads of state, CEOs of corporations, ministers and the judiciary. A major stereotype is that short-term memory is impaired, along with the ability to learn new skills.

While experiments asking subjects to memorize lists of digits or letters are reported to show such a decrement, it should be remembered that memory of meaningful data occurs in a context that helps to reinforce and therefore retain it. Aids such as filofaxes, pocket memos and personal computers can prevent many small effects intruding, if indeed they do. As for learning new skills, motivation is a key element here. What is learned can be related to a framework of valuable experience to help retention, rather being absorbed serially in an uncodified way as younger, inexperienced people may do.

Other stereotypes are more related to the job context and whether older workers will fit in with younger ones, especially if they have to report to them. Experience indicates that this is more to do with personality and clarity of roles rather than merely being a certain age. In service-related industries, older managers can be valuable. According to some employers, age brings experience of dealing with difficult customers, tolerance, conscientiousness and reliability.

There is another assumption that older staff lack drive and will not accept offers equal to or lower than their present salaries. Circumstances can vary so much that it is worth questioning these assumptions. The case of 43-year-old John is a clear example of this. Made redundant from a process manufacturing company, he took a reduction in salary as a production manager for a UK foreign-owned company. It specialized in making aluminium for packaging and containers. John, already a grandfather and with children running their own homes, threw himself energetically into his new job. He was sent away on a senior management programme after a year and, during it, was told he was being considered for a substantial promotion, involving frequent travel abroad. The message here, clearly, is to take each individual on their merits.

The signs are that, while the 40 age barrier is still entrenched in some recruiters' thinking, other organizations are beginning to change. One large national management consultancy, for example, recently advertised for senior consultants up to 45 years where previously it had stipulated 40. The first organizations to have relaxed age requirements were those who had difficulty in recruitment. To illustrate this point, direct entry to the Civil Service grades has crept up from 37 to 52 years of age over the last few years, as an uncompetitive remuneration policy has made the skills shortage worse.

The idea that conventional careers peter out at 45 is also being resisted by various self-help groups such as the Third Age Network and the Association of Retired Persons. The latter's US counterpart has successfully campaigned for changes in legislation regarding age discrimination, pensions and healthcare. There, it has been illegal for over 20 years to put an age bar in recruitment advertising.

6.3 High-flyers and flyers

Another policy that organizations could review from several angles if they are to avoid wasting human resources is that of high-flyers. They are normally those selected for rapid advancement in accordance with the internal career timetables mentioned in Chapter 5 because of their believed future potential value to the organization.

'Potential' is different from 'promotability', which is usually the perceived ability to do a job at the next level up, as it is the likely ultimate position in the organization that an individual will occupy in, say, five or ten years' time. The underlying assumption is that a few individuals will learn and grow quicker than others and that special development and training enhances talent rather than creates it. Within the organization, this can seem at odds with a management development programme that promotes a view that, given sufficient training, managers can do almost anything, and training is seen as a means of remedying deficiencies.

Options for high-flyer policies

Those designated as high-flyers belong to a definite cadre that can be defined in several ways, depending on the organization. For selection into the administrative class of the Civil Service (fast stream) a tough, approximately two-day procedure is used as graduates may have little or no work experience. Intellectual capacity is a prime requirement and suitable stretching and developmental jobs will be found for appointees. Other organizations may also grade applicants on entry (see Chapter 5) to see which individuals merit attention.

Some organizations, such as NatWest, prefer to leave the process until the graduate has had several years' experience so that the prediction of potential is based on an internal track record and current performance.

A third option is to examine the results of appraisal and assessment centres (see Chapter 5) to see which individuals are likely to benefit from such a scheme. A few may then be chosen to study for an MBA or to lead a temporary project team.

Disadvantages

This latter method can be a risky business as it is usually highly visible and related to an important or difficult task. While success is always anticipated, failure can be costly and recovery difficult.

Temporary corporate assignments are not easy to manage as they usually involve coordinating the efforts of those from other departments without any direct authority. Often the manager will not have been prepared for this change in role, with its emphasis on negotiation and influence. Furthermore, in project management, it is difficult to avoid overruns and exceeding the original cost budgets. If failure occurs, it will be a long time before the individual is entrusted with the same degree of responsibility again.

Other problems associated with a high-flyer policy are that it can raise expectations to a very high level and if business circumstances change suddenly, the most highly motivated can turn overnight into the most dissatisfied individuals and leave.

Second, the many 'solid citizens' whose performance is good may find that their own motivational needs and careers are neglected for the sake of the few.

Third, a feeling of élitism or arrogance may be attributed to this select group by others in the organization. They may believe it is more of a self-fulfilling prophecy that these individuals will succeed once they have been identified. Their selectors will not *let* them fail as they would be reluctant to admit that they had made a mistake.

Another problem is that such a cadre identified so early on could exclude those having taken career breaks (usually women) or those who have decided on a switch in career later in life, such as managers who have had very broad experience or have more than one specialism.

Advantages

Advantages claimed for a high-flyer policy are that it creates a controlled pool of managers for ensuring corporate succession. It takes into account incorrect identification of talent (due to lack of ability or motivation), wastage and organizational politics. Unilever, Shell, Procter and Gamble, BP and many other companies have operated these schemes for many decades. Smaller ones have more difficulty in finding the variety of postings to ensure continuity and rapidity of progress over and above the norm.

Second, the existence of such a policy is said to attract good-calibre people, especially if there is the possibility of an MBA with periods of study abroad.

Third, the scheme is seen as a way of sustaining commitment in high performers as they can see that so much is being invested in them by the organization.

6.4 Generalists or multispecialists?

The generalist

The days of the gifted amateur (or generalist) who moved around different parts of the organization are numbered. One former staunch exponent of this policy was the Civil Service. Now, various changes, such as agencies being created, the separation of the policy makers from the operational branches and a move towards decentralization, have all forced a recognition that generalists must focus their skills more sharply in a complex environment.

It used to be said that, as a generalist, all one needed to do was to ask the right questions. Today the reply might be, 'well how are you going to evaluate the answers?' Relying on one's specialist advisers to do this is the counter argument, but it is still simplistic. Managerial decision making is a balancing process and some detailed knowledge or experience gained in different areas helps to assess more closely which are the more important questions to ask in the first place. It also helps to determine what yardsticks should be applied in assessing the answers.

The implication for careers is that people wishing to move between departments or functions not only need open-mindedness, motivation and learning ability, but also support from the organization itself. Specialist knowledge and training are needed to build a platform on which to base the move.

The multispecialist

Being part of a multidisciplinary task force is a useful starting point. It offers exposure to how people in different roles view a problem or issue, what their believed contribution is and what attitudes and problem-solving approaches each uses.

It is useful if these multispecialists can combine time in a line function with one or possibly two other specialisms. Sometimes the bridges can be relatively easily crossed, as in the following example. Joe was an IT specialist who worked on a large-scale manufacturing requirements planning system for three years, doing development and implementation work. Because this system became so fundamental to the organizations' work, he first took over the factory control of the system, bringing him into close contact with marketing planning, finance and accounts, purchasing and distribution. This provided a good base for assuming a production managers' role later on.

Another example of developing multispecialists is in the information management department of a large airline. There, IT professionals are encouraged to spend time in other core business functions, such as marketing and engineering. Again, one large oil company has for a long time required of its sales team an expertise (usually a degree) in a subject directly relevant to its products, as the sales role there is viewed more as one of consultancy and problem solving rather than merely persuading people to buy products.

Information technology and information management are very versatile specialisms as they are increasingly being combined with other, more traditional functions. IT and marketing, for example, are needed to deliver financial products, IT hardware and software and travel services. Alternatively, combined with human resources knowledge, IT is useful for personnel administration systems, payroll, computer-based training and manpower planning. IT and accounting are a good combination for auditing, inventory control and distribution. Finance, accounting and IT can be combined with services in compensation and benefits and personal tax planning. The list is only limited by the variety of skills, professional requirements and individual imagination. Human resource management is another useful background. With the growth in the numbers of knowledge workers who need to be managed and the increase in the size of the service industries, the theory and practice of recruiting, retaining and developing staff provides a useful source of ideas when managers are operating in different contexts.

USING THEIR SKILLS

This need for multispecialists has also been noted by professional firms. One recent advertisement in the national press required solicitors with their own specialist branch of legal knowledge and practice applying it to particular industrial sectors. For example, a solicitor specializing in product litigation for the pharmaceutical industry, another for dispute-based negotiation, arbitration and litigation in the construction industry, and a third to handle intellectual property work for the telecommunications and hi-tech industries.

Clearly the environmental and strategic needs of the organization will be driving factors in allowing these managerial hybrids to flourish. General managers can be an enabling factor in spotting an opportunity for applying such a combination of skills to business needs and bringing these to the attention of their staff.

They are also well-placed to see whether individuals who have developed one or more specialisms can broaden their careers into line or general management jobs.

6.5 Specialists into line managers?

Special problems

An important factor in expanding careers, therefore, is the willingness of the organization to encourage the specialist to grow into operational jobs related to the core business of the organization. Those in specialist functions are likely to plateau early (see Chapter 4) and need to plan for this if they are not to become dissatisfied with what may be seen to be a sudden block on their promotion.

This policy of moving people into new areas and accepting the risks of possible short-term errors as part of the process needs top management commitment. Specialists may be apprehensive of such a move, even if they welcome it as a necessary part of their own development, and they may require reassurance that they will be encouraged, trained and supported. Their host line managers may also require convincing of the value of this for their own department and for the organization as a whole.

An illustration of how important support is concerns information management staff who may have progressed through the traditional route of junior programmer, programmer, systems analyst and senior systems analyst. They may fear the loss of specialist skills if they transfer out of their department for, say, two years. What will their position be if things do not work out satisfactorily? There will not be a successful track record in line management, nor will they have the up-to-date knowledge that returning to their home function demands. What they *will* have is an end-user appreciation of systems and, maybe, knowledge of an application area. The value of this trade-off to career development will need to be carefully assessed by both senior managers and their staff.

To enable this transition to occur, the policy makers and line managers have to understand the orientations, motivations and work habits of specialists. These may appear very different from theirs and seem to indicate a lack of organizational commitment. Specialists may have a stronger loyalty to their professional bodies than to their current employer. This is because they hold particular values about performance and success and the methods by which they are achieved. These may or may not coincide with those of the organization in which they work. For example, technical adequacy of performance may be what is required of a product for a niche market rather than technical supremacy. For a specialist, this can be hard to accept. One saying that was often reported by line managers in a hi-tech multinational was:

Why do we persist in making a Rolls Royce when a mini would do?

This is the type of classic remark to be found in technology-driven rather than market-led cultures. These specialist values continue to be reinforced by the existence of a strong specialist subculture. The latter operates within the overall corporate culture, sometimes to the extent that whole groups of senior managers have to be sent away on programmes to become 'more business aware'.

Individuals may be surrounded by fellow specialists with similar core skills, problem solving patterns and modes of thinking. They may consider themselves special and set apart from the rest, dress and speak differently and have contrasting work patterns. All these things may affect their relations with line managers. The managing director of a small 150-person high growth computer software company put it like this:

> I'm desperately short of creative programmers. They may produce nothing for 20 of the 22 working days in a month. They come in late, go early, dress in pullovers and jeans and may not be very communicative about what they are doing. Then suddenly they will find a breakthrough and work solidly for two days on site, even weekends, and go without sleep as they crack the problem. So the company (and other staff) have to accept this. I was once like that but I had to change as the company grew.

Although an organization may accept on a rational level the need for these special skills, it may be emotionally resistant to them as the majority of managers may lack an understanding of the relevant expertise and have fears about how it can be controlled. There may be a feeling that too many specialists will erode the company culture.

If specialists do become line managers, the values and style of work they will have to adopt will be very different. They will be required to be accountable for business success even when many factors are outside their control. Instead of only having to motivate themselves, they will need to motivate many others to achieve their goals. Success will depend on delegation and maintaining good interpersonal relations and taking decisions in uncertainty. It can seem unprofessional and be uncomfortable for specialists not to be able to obtain an extra piece of information that would contribute to a feeling of professional security. It is also difficult for specialists to give up the application of their technical expertise that has brought them recognition and promotion. They have to derive different forms of enjoyment from their work. Where once they could enthuse over the design qualities of a product, the elegance of a programme or a conference appearance to describe a successful case study, they no longer can. Satisfaction now has to come through contributing to the implementation of the corporate strategy, meeting targets, reducing costs and expanding sales. It may seem that depth has been sacrificed for breadth (or, in their eyes, superficiality) and the need to coordinate many roles. Paperwork may seem endless and the only sense of reward is when it is cleared. This is a contrast to the fulfilment of solving a technical problem or providing a well thought out series of options as professional advice.

Specialists and line managers tend to be suspicious of each other when it comes to evaluating the other's performance. Specialists who find that they are to be managed by a non-specialist believe that their contribution will not be recognized and that even if it is, its significance cannot be evaluated properly. They may feel more comfortable with fellow specialists who can appreciate their difficulties, communicate with them and action their problems. In the reverse situation, the specialist transferred to a line job may be stereotyped as narrow, lacking in experience, impractical, academic, indecisive and so on.

The fact is, however, that individuals who are able to cross organizational boundaries can create new roles and careers for themselves, avoiding the plateau and possible redundancy. Accountants who have not been admitted to partnership are an example. They are in demand as practice managers for architects, lawyers, consultancies and other accountants. They naturally have a detailed knowledge of the operation of all the control data and ratios, possess business skills and the appropriate attitudes. Typically, they are required to control the administration, information management, payroll and human resources functions. This enables the professionals to devote their attention to the clients' and the practices' needs.

The recognition that more flexibility is required in specialist careers is seen, for example, in the concerns of the large firms of consulting engineers. Most engineers work their way up as part of a project team and have little preparation for management before they are asked to lead a team. Moreover, the Engineering Council estimates that about half an engineer's technological knowledge is outdated within five years. This suggests that other career paths, not necessarily involving detailed engineering knowledge need to be opened up if engineers are not to become plateaued. Indeed, at the time of writing, BICC, British Gas and Rolls Royce are headed by former engineers – if any inspiration or examples are needed.

The future

Looking to the future, some of these problems and misconceptions of the specialist and line roles may well ease or even disappear. Drucker[1] foresees the time when these knowledge workers will be directed in task-based, multidisciplinary teams. Therefore the old sequence (as in sectors such as pharmaceuticals, hi-tech and telecommunications) of research, development, manufacturing, marketing and distribution will be replaced by 'synchrony'. That is where all the necessary specialists are brought together early on and work as a team rather than through a fixed sequential structure.

In the meantime, if policies do not exist for enabling specialists to take up other forms of management, the plateauing, demotivation and wastage will continue to occur.

Their paths can be eased, first, by an appreciation of the differences between the specialist and line management roles and by special conversion courses, which exist, for example, in the Civil Service.

Second, they can be monitored and mentored in their new roles and reminded not to slip back into old habits, such as getting involved in specialist or technical problems when someone else should be doing this. Specialists are not used to managing teams and they may need guidance in handling the human resource issues. Requiring them to produce mission statements and plans for their unit is one way to broaden their perspectives. Critical review of such plans enables them to see what their contribution can be to overall performance and will help them communicate more effectively with their teams.

A third major area where existing line managers can have a significant influence is in the development of parallel career paths. In fact, technical and functional specialists in some companies (Honeywell, Esso, Hewlett Packard, ICI and Sandoz) are included in the high-flyers group and are given separate but equal status career paths. Lateral movement is encouraged up to a certain level and, after that, paths are either along the professional or managerial route. The professionals are often leaders in their field and operate in a way that is crucial to the success of the company. Their expertise may not be easy to replace and it is in the company's interest to retain them. However, care must be taken if they are managing other specialists that they do not merely use their position to reserve the interesting projects for themselves.

Critics of this dual career path approach would say that there is never real parity. There are invariably limits set on the professionals' advancement, inequalities exist in pay and fringe benefits and managers in a comparable line position do not consult them on relevant issues. However, until synchrony becomes commonplace, the general manager can consider the three main options to see how best to motivate staff and can influence organizational policies that will help to provide a career path and set realistic criteria for promotion.

6.6 Promotion

When an organization operates its promotion policies, it is first and foremost attempting to control its future. It is entrusting custodianship to managers in key positions to ensure that they protect its interests and maintain its culture. Policies offer yardsticks as to what may be attained, the speed at which this can happen and the limits of the pool into which managers can be promoted. For example, this could be the top 500 in a large airline or the top 200 in an engineering company. The policies indicate the values in the culture by supporting one type of behaviour rather than another and hold up role models of what success is. Currently, emphasis on appraisal systems, competences and graded assessments of promotability are the objective parts of the system, designed to make it appear consistent and fair. One summary of the functions of promotion[2] from an individual perspective is that it:

- stimulates amibition
- explains why things are as they are
- reconciles people to career disappointment.

As always, an informal promotion policy may operate in parallel or even against the official one, based on less formalized criteria. Those who have the right image (such as 'can do', positive, energetic but not stressed, generating confidence in senior management that they will fight their corner) or who operate in the right networks (see Chapter 5) have an advantage in steering their careers in their chosen direction.

Task hierarchies

Attention has been drawn to the structure of work as one influential determinant of promotion policies.[3] In 'task continuous hierarchies', there are clear skill gradations and each successive step encompasses the same base of expertise, only more of it or applied in a more refined way. These people can work on their own account or supervise more junior staff. They tend to be specialists. For example, the hierarchy in an audit team may be the graduate student under contract, the supervisor, manager, senior manager and partner. They gain progressive expertise not only in the professional and legal requirements but with their clients and their clients' sector.

In 'task discontinuous hierarchies', a job may not really overlap with one at the previous lower level and the problem is then one of how to bridge the group of competences in one job with those in another to further one's career.

Culture's effects on promotion

The influence of culture on career has already been described in Chapter 5 and the impact that this has makes it difficult to alter the patterns of promotion. The promotion system as part of the culture determines which functions or types are valued. Therefore, those who conform to these values are promoted and, in turn, serve as role models. Once at the top, these models reinforce the culture that promoted them. It may take the arrival of an external CEO, bringing different values to the organization to break the pattern. Promotability is, thus, still frequently seen as pleasing the boss and many assessment instruments now show how discrepant ratings can be between superior and colleagues on key tasks, such as planning, communication, problem solving and so on.

Future changes

Looking to the future, the patterns may be shifted if peer assessment were to become the norm. If the trend to flatter organizational hierarchies and more team-based work continues, the focus for decision making about promotability will increasingly become colleagues who have a direct and frequent interaction with the individual concerned. Therefore peer relationships will be influential in determining career success in organizational terms and could even extend into the area of compensation and benefits.

6.7 Compensation and benefits

Until recently, promotion and compensation have been seen as being inextricably linked. With the collapse of traditional career ladders based on rungs and the need for the retention of staff through flexibility in rewards and working arrangements, compensation has tended to move away from grading and points systems to performance-related pay. This, plus a range of benefits to cater for individual preferences and motivational patterns according to the life stage the employee has reached, is increasingly seen as the way forward.

Performance-related pay

Performance-related pay may depend on individual, group or company performance. Managers may receive payment based on a combination of all of the three elements.

The link between pay and individual performance varies in the ease with which it can be determined. Sales has typically been an area where individual incentives have been set in order to increase peformance. However, with complex products or services, team and backup support is often vital and consideration needs to be given to these factors when determining rewards. In other functions where output is less directly measurable, performance management techniques and appraisal play a prominent role.

The advantage of performance-related pay is that it allows the organization to direct employees' and their managers' efforts and achievements to where the business requires it. Outstanding performers can more easily be recognized from colleagues who are just satisfactory. This can result in greater involvement in work as employees know that they will be asked to leave if they do not perform. This leads them to seek clarity of objectives, the boundaries of their authority and responsibility, the organization's strategy and the context of their decision making. If there is a requirement for team results (the new forms of organization structure point towards a more group-oriented approach to work) then there is the ability to adjust the individual and team components to encourage this behaviour. Similarly, if part of the performance is to adopt new organizational values or implement a new programme of customer care, this can also be accommodated. Senior managers, therefore, have a vital role in communicating this to staff so that they can take it into account in their career moves.

Fringe benefits

Fringe benefits also enable an organization to fine tune its compensation package. The list of fringe benefits is growing and seems limited only by the organization's ingenuity and the governments' tax policies. Mortgage subsidies, a car, free petrol, low-interest loans, private health care, share option schemes – these are some of the more traditional ones. Others are fitness and club facilities, equipment to work from home and childcare allowances.

Their common aim is, through being innovative, to recruit and retain able staff who will perform well. However, money is not everything and current recruitment and retention problems in some City institutions has been blamed, among other things, on the lack of career development prospects.

Complications

COMPARABLE PAY

Policies on compensation and benefits are further complicated by the overlaid structures and norms of different sectors and functions. For example, the various branches of engineering have plenty of contract staff supplied by agencies. Despite the shortages, pay is lower than for computing staff, large numbers of whom may operate on a freelance basis as well.

Both professions publish annual salary surveys that give an indication of the bands of pay associated with different stages in the professionals' career. Similarly, various merchant banks and City institutions form salary clubs to share information on current rates and expectations for different levels of seniority. Sometimes specialist salaries can be so out of step within the organization that a solution is to take them outside the system and relate their pay to their particular professional body to create a clear rationale for all concerned.

THE INTERNATIONAL DIMENSION

International comparisons can make things even more difficult, especially if a career move for several years is planned. This area has, to some extent, been covered in Chapter 3, but it is worthwhile listing some factors that make comparisons problematic:

- there are many ways of calculating the cost of living
- the relationship between tax and perks varies from country to country: in Germany, commuting costs are tax deductible and in France this applies to childcare, but in the UK neither are
- pay practices differ
- hidden costs may not be comparable, for example, national insurance accounts for about 20 per cent of salary in Germany, but in the UK it is only 9 per cent
- managers' perceptions vary, for instance, French and German people may not be attracted to working in the UK as their total pay may look much smaller, but if their housing were paid for by the company, the buying power of the salary would appear much more favourable.

Making decisions

Balancing perceptions, needs, compensation packages and careers is a delicate and individualistic matter and it is difficult to offer any specific guidelines. General managers cannot automatically assume that they know the combinations of factors that will motivate their subordinates – they need to get to know them and ask them. Second, they will benefit from being confident that their organizational policies on compensation and benefits are clear and yet flexible enough to meet specific organizational needs. If they are still seen as barriers to be overcome, then they probably need to explain the position and negotiate with the human resources function to make sure that the appropriate career decisions can be made.

6.8 Corporate development programmes

There are other incentives for employees to perform and manage their own careers apart from the various compensation and benefits packages. Opportunities for self-development (thereby enhancing internal and external marketability and career prospects) are one of these key incentives. If the organization has set up a corporate development programme for certain of its staff, this can be a catalyst for career thinking. These programmes are not necessarily for high-flyers (Sainsburys uses them for its executives aged around 35 years as an aid to career development) and the very decision about whether or not to apply can cause some critical self-analysis.

MBAs

The programmes, in some cases, will be tailored or intercompany MBAs.

Terminology varies according to the institution, but a tailored MBA is generally designed for specific companies, such as Shell, BICC, John Brown Engineering and Grand Met, that have a large enough intake to operate as separate courses over several years. These usually have all the standard disciplines built in, such as operations management, finance, marketing, human resources and so on, but may incorporate specially designed industry-specific case studies, workshops or elective studies. That way, the needs of the organization can be met, confidentiality guaranteed and the corporate culture reinforced.

Action learning is easy to arrange for participants as access to the course does not have to be negotiated in the same way as with an outside college, say. Participants also spend the minimum time away from work. Skills acquired can be implemented quickly and consistency and continuity with other courses can be arranged. Internal company personnel can be used as tutors and facilitators for certain subjects, thereby enhancing credibility and involving these senior managers in future staff development. Other benefits claimed are that working relationships across functions are improved.

Intercompany MBAs, as they are often called, seek to retain some of the advantages of a tailored programme while broadening their participants' thinking. Usually, they are for those companies that are not large enough to warrant participation in a tailored course or only wish to send five or so delegates at a time. They are thus able to use this as a means of retaining some control over what is taught and how.

From the start, participants are in mixed groups and projects or dissertations can be done in each others' organizations, enabling members to contrast different practices and cross-fertilize ideas.

Motivation has to be very high for these programmes to succeed. The participants will need to be committed enough to give up evenings and weekends to private study and assignment preparation for two or three years. It is therefore a decision that involves not just the company but the whole family. Because of the level of challenge involved, offering MBAs is one way of motivating young managers or those who are plateaued but are, none the less, valuable to the company.

If the MBA sounds too daunting, a less demanding programme of certificates and diplomas may be undertaken. These will provide a management qualification that can, in some cases be used later, if required, to gain exemption from certain of the course components of an MBA or be used in bridge-building for a possible change in career.

6.9 Sponsoring individual qualifications

For those not covered by a formal company scheme, sponsorship may be used by senior managers as an individual reward or as a recruitment tool for current or future staff. For example, newly qualified graduates are attracted to large organizations by the possibility of such sponsorship for an MBA after five years or so. The arrangements can be highly flexible: full- or part-time, modular or via distance learning. Attractiveness is further enhanced by the possibility of obtaining exemptions from selective examinations of various professional bodies, such as the Institute of Marketing.

Disadvantages

Nevertheless, there is some ambivalence towards the holders of MBAs. Criticisms often levelled at them are the expectations of over-inflated salaries, arrogance and lack of commitment to the organization. There is also the fear that, once qualified, at considerable expense to the company (although European and USA fees for degrees are several times more expensive than those in the UK), they will leave. Others would argue that loyalty may be *increased* or that the organization can stipulate as a condition of sponsorship that the MBA graduate stays a minimum of two years with the organization after qualifying.

Advantages

The advantage of an MBA is that it can prepare its holder for promotion by providing a multifunctional and strategic perspective on issues and problems that may not be present in the current job.

Other spin-offs are the increasing emphasis on internationalism and the acquiring of skills like presentation, leadership, interpersonal and foreign languages and so on during the programme. The project-based assignments can also save the company money that would have had to be spent on external consultants.

Having received a training of this scope, retention of these graduates will be difficult if their jobs do not stretch them or if functional boundaries within the organization are too tightly drawn and defended to allow some flexibility of operation. These are areas that general managers can influence to provide a basis on which career experience can be broadened.

6.10 Open learning

Open learning facilities provided by the organization can also enhance personal effectiveness and offer new awareness for career development. This is advantageous in that individuals do not feel pressurized and can take the learning at their own pace, according to their needs.

Computer-based training, interactive video, language training and general interest lunchtime seminars are all examples of this. If the organization has already invested in an infrastructure of IT, then the provision of opportunities is greatly expanded, as was done with the then Austin Rover Group.

Provision of access to high-quality training for large numbers of people increases the critical mass for creating the learning organization, with its emphasis on self-development. The disadvantage may be that there is no transferable qualification for the individual at the end. However, motivation can still be recognized and rewarded through appraisal and by the opening up of other opportunities for career development.

Open learning facilities are an area that need the support of senior managers if they are to flourish. They require an investment of time and money that may not be directly returned in an individual's current job, although it could facilitate their career.

6.11 Career break schemes

Career break schemes are another policy area to which employers are giving attention as they offer both senior managers and their staff additional flexibility in working arrangements. They may be added to traditional compensation and benefits packages as a way of recruiting and retaining staff and providing a pool of temporary labour. They are also a means of granting time off work, usually to care for children in addition to the statutory maternity and paternity leave that some firms allow.

Employers' individual schemes vary but can cover men and women employees of all grades (as with Esso) for an absence of up to five years with guarantees of normal benefits and a job on their return. Another scheme, offered by Barclays Bank, allows staff to retain their pensions, low-cost home loans and so on. Organizations also differ in their qualifying requirements (say, from one to three years' service) and whether the time can be used to care for elderly relatives.

The period of absence is unpaid and there are a variety of mechanisms for keeping employees in touch. NatWest offers seminars, updates, newsletters, two weeks' compulsory employment and attendance at training schemes. Companies such as BP and Boots also implement such schemes, the latter maintaining a returners' network of support and information.

Specific schemes for women

At a more general level, there are a number of initiatives and interest groups specifically focusing on women returners. The governments' Training Agency is developing a system to provide advice from a computer database about training, education and career opportunities that will be made available at certain locations in the UK. Various professional bodies (for whose members general managers may have some responsibility) are examining the issues and implications involved in career break schemes. The Institute of Chartered Accountants in England and Wales is trying to encourage a more supportive attitude to women wishing to combine a family and career. So, too, are the Law Society and the British Medical Association as more than half those training to be doctors are women.

In another initiative, professional women engineers, scientists and technologists are being encouraged to return to senior management jobs in manufacturing by studying at university while being employed part-time by the company. This scheme is being funded by the Training Agency and is planned to lead to an MSc in manufacturing management. The rationale is that it is estimated that in the UK some 5000 women are not making use of their degrees and that it costs between £20 000 and £40 000 to educate a graduate engineer.

Another type of scheme is for organizations to form a consortium, paying an annual fee and sponsoring two or more returners (men or women). In return, a consultancy offers to recruit and train the returners on a four-week course. Companies (B&Q, Tesco, Thorn EMI, Pizza Hut and Network South East to name but a few) then offer a six-week period of work experience, without obligation for employment for either party.

The picture would not be complete without making some European comparisons. In general, various draft directives from the EC share the view that men and women are equally responsible for childcare and therefore parents of either sex should be entitled to a career break, taken separately from any maternity or paternity leave granted.

Most European countries have introduced some schemes to minimize career disruption to women. In Sweden, parental leave was introduced over 17 years ago. One years' leave is granted and extended accordingly if a part-time arrangement is made for employment. Benefits are paid by the state so employers stand the opportunity cost of employing that person and the cost of replacing them.

Whether or not they think such schemes are what they want in their own organizations, senior managers will increasingly be asked questions about them. They will need to decide how and whether they can be accommodated in their own particular operation.

6.12 Child and family care provision

Child and family care provision is another area where policies can affect individuals' career chances. They help to increase retention and create an image of flexibility on the part of the firm. The need for such schemes is that the main reason preventing the estimated one million women returners from taking up employment is the availability of childcare for various ages.

There are some 3.5 million children under 5 years old and state-run nurseries cater for only 35 000 of them, which is about 1 per cent. It is estimated that approximately a further 100 000 of them receive individual care from nannies and au pairs and another 3000 have workplace provision. Demand clearly outstrips supply.

For many parents who may be willing to work, the cost of childminders or other care outweighs their earnings or takes up so much of it that employment ceases to be a cost-effective option. There are also few after-school schemes for the supervision of older children. With an increase in the number of single parents (now about 1.1 million), the need for help with childcare is likely to become more urgent.

The options for employers

A number of possibilities exist for assistance with childcare:

– workplace nurseries
– employer-subsidized nurseries

CAREER-LINKED ORGANIZATIONAL POLICIES 155

- firms employing childminders
- voucher schemes and financial assistance
- collaboration with schools and local authorities
- special leave and flexible working.

There are pros and cons with each of the options and some organizations will create their own variants to suit their circumstances.

The generosity of their provision is likely to depend on several factors: how critical the shortage of staff is, business strategy, geographical location and multisite organization and the overall attitude to staff – whether the company sees its employees as a cost or an investment, to be nurtured in as many ways as possible.

WORKPLACE NURSERIES

Workplace nurseries have been in the spotlight ever since the Midland Bank announced that it intended to set up 300 of them to attract and retain women staff (it employs some 20000 women). Other well-known names doing this are Unilever, TSB, Sears, DEC, Trust House Forte, Thomas Cook, Grand Met, Sainsburys, British Airways and Aquascutum. All sectors appear to be interested.

As for the staff themselves, not all parents are willing to take their children on what could be for some a long and tiring journey across a major city in the rush hour. One father who used to do this regularly said,

> It can be positively dangerous. On one occasion the train was so crowded that I was pushed towards the side of the carriage and my nine-month-old child's hand was closed in the door.

Others may be working unsocial hours or travel extensively and find the core provision for childcare inadequate.

Moreover, if an organization is multisite it is not possible to designate one location as 'the site' for a nursery in order to maximize the utilization and cost-effectiveness. The set-up costs are high, especially if a multidisciplinary team of childcare professional, consultant and internal managers is involved and a survey of employees' preferences is carried out. Then there is the expense of the acquisition of suitable premises, which have to conform to a number of environmental and safety criteria. In addition, there is the recruitment and payment of trained staff, present in the correct ratio to satisfy local authority requirements and to cover for sickness. Excluding the acquisition of premises, estimates for setting up a 24-place nursery seem to be fairly consistent at around £25000 to £35000. Running costs are usually at least £100 per child per week, with employers paying ⅔ and the employee the rest. Now that this is no longer a taxable benefit for employees, more firms may consider it worthwhile. The dilemma still remains, however, about what happens when a child is ill or has to remain in quarantine with the usual ailments that are so common in the pre-school child.

EMPLOYER-SUBSIDIZED NURSERIES

An alternative to the workplace nursery is one that the employer subsidizes, such as the bank Merril Lynch and the Prudential schemes. This has the advantage of not necessarily being restricted to a particular location and avoids the initial costs. If demand falls, then the employer does not feel obliged to keep the overhead going. Also, several employers, perhaps with local branch offices, have the opportunity to share the nursery with other companies, thus avoiding the cost of using expensive business space.

COMPANY-EMPLOYED CHILDMINDERS

Firms may also employ childminders for their staff but are at present unable to write off such costs against tax. Nor can they employ other forms of domestic help, such as a nanny or a cleaner and claim relief as they can for an office cleaner or a secretary. The logic of this is not consistent and the philosophy not supportive for managing careers.

Progress on these fronts is hampered by the continuing debate over who should pay – government, employer or employee – for what some would say is for the good of the national economy. Others would argue that allowing organizations tax relief is passing the burden onto the taxpayers who will use the services.

VOUCHER SCHEMES AND FINANCIAL ASSISTANCE

Voucher schemes and financial packages are other inducements.

Vouchers (pioneered by Luncheon Vouchers Limited) can be personalized for parents to help with the costs of childcare. They are taxable, but exempt from national insurance. This ensures that the extra money can be spent *only* on childcare (avoiding possible antagonism from other employees) and creates a benefit of equal external value to high-earning and low-earning employees alike. The childcarer, who must be legally allowed to look after children, signs an agreement with the company supplying the vouchers. These are signed by both employees and childcarers and are redeemable by the voucher company within, say, five working days.

Firms using such schemes are KPMG Peat Marwick (management consultants) and National Power.

Other forms of assistance are special subsidies to working mothers. Abbey National is offering to women (11000 of its employees are women) a bonus of £75 per month for the first two years back in the office after childbirth. Similarly, Legal and General will pay women an extra 25 per cent on top of their normal salary for six months.

All these schemes offer both managers and their staff flexibility and choice.

COLLABORATION WITH SCHOOLS AND LOCAL AUTHORITIES

This is another option, especially where children are older but still need supervision.

These arrangements are of interest to the major clearing banks since their national branch networks draw on the local labour markets. Grand Met, having introduced workplace nurseries, still found that only a small proportion of its women managers (numbering in their hundreds) entered senior management, so they are examining ways of seeing that older children (aged 5 to 14) are looked after in the holidays, as is National Savings.

SPECIAL LEAVE AND FLEXIBLE WORKING

Firms offering paid leave for looking after sick children are Unilever, RMC Group, Royal Bank of Scotland, Marks and Spencer, Sears and BP. Furthermore, unpaid leave to care for children in the holidays is granted by British Telecom, BA, ICI and Grand Met.

Other organizations run job sharing schemes, including Shell International, Lloyds Bank, GEC and British Gas, and Boots offers jobs where the working day coincides with school hours.

Care of the elderly

Another area that is beginning to receive attention is the care of the elderly. There are reputedly 6 million people who look after elderly relatives and at least 10 per cent of them also have full-time or part-time jobs. About 3.5 million are women and 2.5 are men, yet few employers do anything to help.

There is a particular problem here for women as middle age is the time when children may be growing up but still be at home and elderly parents start to make demands. With increasing longevity, the younger generation will be expected to return the care and support they once had as children.

Individuals tend to use up annual leave for short-term crises, employers usually reserving compassionate leave for terminal illness. Yet, care for the elderly may be a long-term commitment, falling between these two extremes.

According to one source,[4] about 15 per cent of adults are carers and 25 per cent of these are between 45 and 64. They may themselves be under stress. The symptoms of lack of productivity – fatigue, poor concentration, lateness and absenteeism – that they may exhibit are similar to those resulting from alcohol abuse. The latter symptom attracts the organization's attention and is also a focus for remedial action. It may, therefore, also be the case that parentcare vouchers will have to be offered, alongside ones for childcare, to maintain effectiveness at work.

There are some signs that these problems are being taken seriously. The care of the elderly is a responsibility that some firms (through their retirement schemes) are taking seriously. Pilkingtons, for example,[5] provides a welfare programme involving a range of cash benefits to retired employees given at Christmas, birthdays and retirement. Care is provided to help pensioners who are financially insecure, as is relief for the carers themselves. IBM in the USA provides nationwide telephone assistance to help employees help their elderly relatives wherever they may be.

The lesson from these cases is that senior managers may stand to gain more in the long-term by taking an interest in their staffs' domestic circumstances. If ignored, these might cause a decrement in work performance that could have been avoided.

6.13 Workplace counselling

The stresses of private life, caring for children and relatives, on top of those usually experienced at work, can, in some cases, prove unbearable if they continue long enough. If the general manager as counsellor (see Chapter 4) cannot handle the situation or the GP or occupational nursing staff do not have the time and the training, it is not acceptable for the situation to continue. An inefficient employee for long periods of time can start to cause a knock-on effect of poor morale and an overloaded team. Remedial action taken early enough can prevent not only the manager from having a broken career but also the boss, whose unit's performance will suffer. The rationale is that a happy and balanced employee will be more productive and reliable. Firms are therefore increasingly recognizing the costs of stressed and demotivated staff and feel able to offset them with workplace counselling.

Reasons cited[6] for the growth of the workplace counselling service are based on what has been happening in the USA. Ideas filter through their foreign subsidiaries to become part of UK practice.

First, legislation in the USA holds employers responsible at work not only for the physical safety of employees but also for emotional distress. Second, the incidence of alcoholism, drug abuse and other reactions to stress are becoming increasingly costly (as they are in the UK), with estimates of up to 40 million days being lost through stress-related illnesses. Third, health insurance companies are charging higher insurance premiums in response to the increase in benefits they have to pay out. Reductions are being made in premiums for those running employee counselling services. Add to these the environmental changes outlined in Chapter 2 and the consequential restructuring and alteration in social conditions and there is considerable pressure to examine how all this can affect employees in adverse ways and to see what can be done about it.

In-house counselling

The Post Office is a pioneer in this area and has completed a successful three-year trial.[7] It already had an occupational health scheme and offered some counselling support through its nursing staff. The aim of the new service was to deal with more complex problems that previously had been referred outside.

Psychiatric and psychological disturbance was reported as being the second main reason for medical retirement. Another feature was that it was recognized that the organization policies and procedures could themselves be a source of stress and therefore aggregate feedback could influence the development and implementation of such policies and the training of those with managerial responsibilities.

The service was located within the occupational health service with similar ethics of confidentiality. If any disclosure was to take place it had to be, 'in the client's interests and with his or her permission or not at all'.

The reported referral pattern was as follows:

- occupational health department, 40 per cent
- self, 31.5 per cent
- welfare, 19 per cent
- other, 9.5 per cent.

Those who were seen came from right across the organization, with different functional groupings and levels represented: postmen, engineers, senior management and so on. The balance of men to women was 73 per cent to 27 per cent, reflecting the proportions in the organization as a whole. Some 25 per cent of requests were seen the same day and a further 25 per cent within 5 days. This prompt action avoided possible deterioration of the situation. The average number of interviews per person referred was 3 and 75 per cent of cases did not require subsequent referral outside the company.

External counselling

Other companies may choose to operate with an external agency, specializing in offering counselling services either because they believe it is the best way for them or because their size does not justify the presence of full-time staff appointments.

The Royal Bank of Canada runs such a service, which has around an 8 per cent take up. They believe it to be more acceptable if individuals have very personal problems for these to be handled outside the company. The company maintains that it benefits from a fresh look at the situation and they can also make comparisons with employees from other companies. The programme also extends to employees' families and pensioners as they may be part of the problem or have some other interest in its resolution. With this type of service, a personnel manager will refer individuals outside, if asked, and employees are allowed a specific number of visits without further payment by the company.

In other situations, employees can ring a number directly themselves without any one else in the company knowing that they have done so. Some 15000 American companies are reported to run such a service.

The companies are provided with statistical data by the agency about the overall level of use, type of problems referred to them and whether they tend to be work-related or have other origins. If the company is large and has several sites, the number of contacts made could also be included as useful management information.

Costs and benefits data are hard to come by as this is a relatively new idea in the UK. The external services are said to be priced at around £40 per employee per annum. To this must be added management and supervisory training and the information and presentations needed to sustain this.

Benefits that can be monitored from the company's own records are typically[8] at least a 50 per cent reduction in lateness, accidents, injury, medical visits, sickness benefits, surgical costs, disciplinary actions and terminations.

Minimum returns on investment seem to be about 2:1 and there are intangible benefits, concerned with image (internal and external) and reduced interpersonal conflict.

Focusing help

Companies may vary in the focus of their referral services (sometimes called employee assistance programmes). Whitbread has a phone-in service to cover its 26000 employees, Johnson and Johnson has a psychotherapist available, Marconi and Aer Lingus have services to deal with alcohol and drug abuse, GEC has a counsellor who trains others in dealing with alcoholics, ICI has nurses trained to counsel people to stop smoking and a large management consultancy gives its managing consultants a self-administered stress inventory and reading material. It is felt that they can better understand stress in themselves and seek help if necessary through the firm's doctor. Abbey Life Building Society, as a result of experiencing a rise in the number of armed raids, has set in motion a new policy for handling the affer-effects. It trains its managers in helping victims and gives them access to an occupational health specialist.

Outside assistance to firms can also come from nationally recognized bodies such as Relate so that the full range of problems can be tackled. Senior managers in organizations using these policies for dealing with work problems are better placed to avoid or reduce these problems, which could otherwise damage their staff's, and possibly their own, careers.

6.14 Conclusion

The career-linked policies cited here that focus on organizational aspects can, if not sensitively handled, become constraints and demotivators to staff. Those that focus on the individual can enable them to grow and overcome weaknesses or personal difficulties which would otherwise stand in the way of career progress.

General managers may therefore think it wise to influence these various policies as they will enable or constrain what they are aiming to do for and with their own managers. Access to a range of policies that can be applied in a flexible way, either singly or in combination, will be vital to the general managers' ability to motivate, develop and retain staff. This, in turn, will affect their ability to meet their own objectives and should prompt them to monitor the management of their own careers.

Action questions

SENIOR MANAGERS

What organizational policies does your organization have that affect careers?
What management implications do they have?

MANAGERS

Are you interested in some of the policies mentioned in this chapter? How might they help your career?

HUMAN RESOURCE SPECIALISTS

When did you last review some of the policies in this chapter?
Might they need to be adapted to help senior managers deal more flexibly with their staff?

References

1. Drucker, P., *The New Realities*, Heinemann, 1989.
2. Sofer, C., *Men in Mid-Career*, Cambridge University Press, 1970.
3. Offe, C., *Industry and Inequality*, Edward Arnold, 1967.
4. Worman, D., 'The Forgotten Carers', *Personnel Management*, January 1990.
5. Worman, D., op. cit.
6. Reddy, M., *The Manager's Guide to Counselling at Work*, BPS and Methuen, 1987.
7. Allinson, T., C. Cooper and P. Reynolds, 'Stress Counselling in the Workplace: the Post Office Experience', *The Psychologist*, September 1989.

7
Individual career planning and development

7.1 Introduction

However much general managers are facilitators or problem solvers or however well they understand their own organizational policies and processes, there can be no substitute for self-help on the part of their staff. This chapter aims to help general managers understand what is involved in helping individuals to help themselves by alerting them to the concepts, tools and techniques available. At the same time, an appreciation of this can throw light on why and how individuals choose various options and perform in what might appear to be a very illogical or inconsistent way.

Individuals vary in their attitudes to the notion of career planning. Some wrestle with a feeling of purposelessness, asking 'where do I go from here?', and will welcome the offer of frameworks, tools and techniques. Others are content with their situation, maintaining that they have never planned their careers and therefore there is no need to start now. A few maintain that it is luck, happening to be at the right place at the right time, and that, however much planning is done, things cannot be made to happen. Yet another group believe that those who do say they benefit from planning are merely rationalizing their experiences. To the cynics, one might put the question 'Is this the random way you would go about buying your next car or running your operational units?'

A theme that has emerged in the last four chapters is that work cannot be insulated from what goes on at home and vice versa. Career and personal life interweave and condition choices, motives and the ability to follow through certain career paths and themes.

Personality influences career choice and occupations because values, beliefs and standards produce certain distinct patterns of behaviour. The concepts and methods for self-assessment help to put individuals in touch with their thinking by making it explicit. This happens through various exercises, completing different inventories of preferences and values and taking many psychometric personality questionnaires. The individual, sometimes with the help of a career counsellor, attempts to identify common threads and to simultaneously relate all this to past, present and future career. Access to databases and personal networks also provide information and a means of evaluating it to move the decision making and action plan forward. As the plans are self-generated and based on information produced and absorbed by the individual, there is likely to be more commitment to them and a stronger motivation to follow them through.

7.2 Life stages and career

When managers plan their careers, they do so in relation to the particular life stage they are at. Writers have tended to see these stages as an unfolding set of sequential periods, marked by alternate phase of transition, conflict and stability. The phases each have their own values, rewards and constraints. Different writers postulate varying numbers of stages in the occupational career (the most the author has seen is nine) that overlap with the major life stages of marriage, birth of first child and children leaving home.

Middle age has typically been seen as a time when peoples' occupational decisions are then set for life: the family has grown up and the couple are forced to re-examine their relationship in preparation for retirement. Experience of various social changes (see Chapter 2) tells us that this traditional pattern is altering, that new family units may be created with a second marriage and that individuals may strike out in new career directions.

One model

The simplest general exposition,[1] based on a study of managers, outlines three stages, based on age:

- launching the career – 25–35
- turning to private life – 35–45
- integrating professional and private life – 45–55.

However, it may be wiser to accept only the phases as the ages associated with them are very variable in reality.

At each phase there are preoccupations. Starting out means that commitment is high (even if failure is encountered) and continuous striving will occur. Success breeds further opportunities to demonstrate even more success and so the striving pattern continues, with ever more mountains to climb.

'Private life' may be interpreted as supporting work rather than the reverse, until a choice or crisis point is reached. It is here that the major private values reassert themselves and a questioning takes place – how to pursue a career without destroying family or personal life, for example. The survey showed that when asked if they had made a sacrifice of the family for the sake of their career, those under 35 years old tended to deny this as they saw their efforts as being for the *benefit* of the family. Those between 35 and 45 years old tended to say 'yes', including the most successful. The second stage is therefore marked by a re-evaluation of the importance of the family role.

Stage three is the integration of work and personal life.[2] Managers and their wives were asked to characterize the relationship between home and work using the following classification:

- *spillover*: one affects the other in a positive or negative way
- *independence*: they exist side by side and seem independent of each other
- *conflict*: they cannot be easily reconciled
- *instrumentality*: one is primarily a means of obtaining something desired in the other
- *compensation*: one makes up for what is missing in the other.

The most common answer was the spillover effect, described by 45 per cent followed by the others in the order listed above. There were also some combinations: spillover and instrumentality and spillover and conflict. The evidence suggests that there is a relationship between work states and private life.

Spillover occurs mainly where the manager is struggling to be successful and is tense and insecure. There may be such a strong need for promotion that the manager dare not say 'no' to any request in case it indicates a lack of skill or an inability to cope. Pressure mounts, work is brought home and social engagements are cancelled.

The independence relationship is one of equilibrium as the manager derives satisfaction from his or her career without feeling that it is a struggle or that there is undue stress.

Conflict, the third reaction, is likely to occur when the manager is very successful, satisfied and stressed, but by excitement, rather than this being a negative pressure, and so is overinvolved with his or her career.

When instrumentality or compensation occur, the manager has switched off from the career or is dissatisfied with work and accepts that there will be no further progress.

This third stage concludes with managers coming to terms with their own limitations and aspirations, coupled with a sense of there being a finite amount of time left to achieve personal objectives. This may be accompanied by a sudden interest to do, say, voluntary work where their management skills can be applied, taking up an entirely new interest or reviving an old one.

Specialists

Career stages apply in a more specific way to specialists. The difference in orientation between specialist or professional roles and the managerial ones was highlighted in Chapter 6. A study of successful professionals[3] in engineering, science, accounting and academic life showed that a prerequisite for success was the passage through four career stages involving different attitudes, behaviours and relationships.

The apprenticeship stage – stage 1 – is learning about the organization and working at the junior tasks.

When competence has been developed, the next relationship is that of colleague – stage 2. There is a recognition of one's contribution to the organization's work as a whole and, at around 30 years, niche specialisms are selected, which are technical or application areas.

It is at this point that the seeds for later blocking are sown. The individual becomes so interested in the specialism that the influencing aspects of being a mentor – stage 3 – at around 35 and directing the work of other specialists may be forgotten. Ironically, the greater the technical and professional success at this stage, the harder it may be to move on. Scientists or professionals may take great pride in being nationally known experts. The later stages may therefore be seen as a reduction in status due to a dilution of expertise, even if this is accompanied by greater financial reward. This third stage brings into play more social skills than before: there is the need to sell the importance of the group's work internally and externally, whereas before it was not so necessary. Such activity would have previously been seen as preaching to the converted.

The fourth and final stage is that of being a sponsor, which coincides with the mid-life transition. Here the focus is on strategic direction and innovation in the organization. Attention must then be paid to politics, power, business needs and resource allocation. The specialist has, in effect, become part of the senior management pool in the organization.

Women

Interestingly enough, there does not appear to be a model for integrating the career and life stages for women. Many women in professional and specialist areas wait until they are approaching the colleague stage at, say, around 30 years to have their first child. If they do not return almost immediately, they miss the important consolidation stage of being accepted and recognized by their peers. If a second child is wanted, it is unlikely that women will be able to break out of this colleague stage into a mentoring role. Influencing relationships will have been disrupted, if only temporarily, and mobility will now be restricted. To rebuild these relationships on return to work, it is vital to move to the mentoring stage, but this may be five to ten years later than the equivalent time period for men, making it unlikely that the women will become sponsors.

One can retrain and encourage women returners at the late colleague stage but no amount of training can substitute for building a network of relationships and influence. The latter may involve considerable and continuous time and effort. It is not surprising, then, that women in their early to mid thirties are faced with a difficult decision. The consequences at the present time remain almost irretrievable: have a family and almost certainly be limited in career opportunity or take the gamble that the mentoring stage *will* be reached, but accept that the chances of having a child will then be almost non-existent. Those that manage to combine family life *and* maintain career progress usually still have the added responsibility for organizing childcare, medical and social matters for the family. They may, therefore, be more concerned about the interactions between family and work life and the demands the latter make on them. The importance for them of spotting and selecting opportunities therefore becomes crucial.

7.3 Choosing opportunities

Although there are many theories about career choice, the majority were built around the older adolescent or young adult. There was an unspoken assumption, consistent with the old theories about organizational stability, that a choice, once made, led inexorably down certain paths. Therefore, until 1975 when organizations were beginning to see an accelerating rate of change, the choices facing the mature adult received scant attention. It is nevertheless worth reviewing the theories as they do provide useful frameworks that, singly or in combination, may help to explain why some managers opt for one type of job rather than another.

A useful classification of theories[4] is that of 'matching' models, where correct fit indicates the soundness of the career choice and subsequent adjustment, and 'process' models which focus on personal development and change.

The matching models

These are the theories concerned with:

- interests and abilities
- self-concept
- needs
- environment.

INTEREST AND ABILITY THEORIES

With the interest and ability theories, the assumption is that people will choose the sort of work about which they are really enthusiastic and for which they have the skills.

The dictionary of occupational titles in the USA fits easily with such an assumption and indicates that elements are included in a job (people, data and things). Therefore, an individual may say that he or she took a job or continued in a career because 'I liked dealing with people'. The difficulty here is that this covers a multitude of meanings: persuading people; caring for them; managing them; advising them and so on.

Some recruiters or careers advisers, to avoid this, fine tune the method by using procedures that involve asking a candidate to indicate a preference for doing specialized tasks with people. A good match would, among other things, be contingent upon the strength of preference for the particular 'people' element being present in the current job, backed by an ability to do it. Problems will obviously occur where people have a strong interest but lack the abilities to perform adequately. The reverse is also true: an individual may have an ability such as strong administrative skills but show little interest in exercising them.

SELF-CONCEPT THEORIES

With self-concept theories, individuals are said to be drawn to occupations that are consistent with the way they see themselves and are reinforced by the image others have of them. The kind of justification given for a career choice could be:

> I see myself as creative and artistic, therefore it would be a waste of my talents not to enter advertising where I can exercise those abilities. Everybody says that.

Another person might say:

> I'm young, dynamic, thrive on change, have plenty of stamina. Consultancy attracts people like that and that's obviously the life for me for a while.

The danger here is that either the self-concept or the job or both may be idealized to the point that a suitable choice is not made. Disillusionment may then set in rapidly when there is a mismatch between the expectation of the job or career and the reality.

NEEDS THEORIES

The needs and wants theories imply a type of check-list approach. Some people may have a very strong need for power and achievement. One man in his mid thirties, when asked what he wanted from his career replied:

> I just need to manage. I enjoy taking on more and more responsibility and seeing people achieve things.

The function was irrelevant – computing, industrial engineering, materials management were all areas in which he had held a line function. Success was controlling an empire. The logistics of this fascinated him while meeting his need for power.

ENVIRONMENT THEORIES

The rationale for the environmental approach is that individuals will choose an environment in which they feel comfortable. This does not mean an unchallenging one, merely that they will feel at ease with the overall purpose and values associated with the job and organization (the corporate culture, discussed in Chapter 5).

Those, for example, with a strong ethical and conservationist approach will feel out of place and antagonistic to a chemical plant that is contributing to pollution by discharging its effluent into rivers. Again, those with a strong theoretical and conceptual approach to problems will feel stifled by a short-term cost-benefit approach, driven by criteria that are continuously and uncritically applied.

The process models

On the other hand, the process models look at careers over time and are classified as follows:

– maturation
– decision analysis

– work adjustment
– social forces.

MATURATION THEORIES

The theories assume that the developing person has to successfully negotiate successive developmental processes in order to deal competently with the various problems that arise. Individuals may fantasize about various jobs and associated lifestyles, then test out the reality accompanying the choice.

On average, at the age of 32, the exploration period finishes and a choice has usually been made.[5] The changes involved in all this experimentation have to cease, otherwise the individual may not be thought to be serious about having a career. On the other hand, if this life stage is reached too quickly, individuals may obtain a false sense of security. An early decision may later trap them because they have never considered or experienced any alternatives. In contrast, those who have wasted too much time exploring false avenues may find that success comes much later (or not at all) depending on the cultural values of the organization.

Selection interviewers have a tendency to look for a consistent, chronological sequence of jobs when candidates apply for a post to identify what may seem, in their eyes, to be drifters.

Again, inventories have been devised to measure occupational maturity by examining the individual's ability to cope with various problems at each stage. The importance of the concept of maturity is borne out by the frequency with which it is used in discussing the suitability of executives for promotion. It often implies a combination of problem solving behaviour, initiative, emotional resilience, emotional control and perseverance. All these are vital in dealing with changes at work.

DECISION ANALYSIS

Decision analysis frameworks focus on how a career choice is formulated and executed. The preferences and willingness to take risks are said to be combined by the individual into a logical, careful assessment of whether to aim high and risk failure or to go for a lower level but relatively safe option. If the latter does not turn out to be successful, all is not lost and can be retrieved without a reduction in self-esteem.

The key concepts here for minimizing risks are exploration (targeted within a defined area) and anticipatory socialization (thinking and behaving as if one has been promoted or given a new role). The latter allows the individual to mentally rehearse being in situations and imagine how they can be dealt with, using observations of behaviour of managers who are successful.

WORK ADJUSTMENT THEORIES

These theories see the individual in a continuous search for job satisfaction, which may be made up from a number of components. When a person moves from one job to the next and is confronted with unfamiliar circumstances, this is said to cause discomfort as old ways of behaving are no longer adequate (see Chapter 3). There follows a period of reorientation when new skills, attitudes and values are required and their acquisition leads to an adaptation, a derivation of satisfaction and good performance in the new role.

It is these theories that generate the idea that a satisfied worker is a productive worker. It is also argued that the reverse is true: being a productive or successful worker brings its own satisfaction and therefore reinforces the drive towards having a job that produces these feelings.

THEORIES ABOUT SOCIAL FORCES

Finally, there is a view that the social forces around us drive us consciously or unconsciously towards various careers.

These forces start at home, in the family and in school. Those figures who have a particular significance in our lives may encourage certain values about which occupations are acceptable for the sons and daughters of certain socio-economic groupings. For example, the established professions of medicine, law, accountancy and so on have traditionally provided career ambitions for the children of socio-economic groupings A and B. They may also be associated with a certain desired status and lifestyles in the community. Demographics, the type of educational opportunities available, and sectoral and skills shortages within certain parts of the country will further condition the extent to which such aspirations are realized.

POPULARITY OF THE THEORIES

It is interesting to note that the appraisal system and assessment centre methodologies that have been growing in popularity in recent years concentrate more on the matching than the process theories. One reason may be that the components of the process theories are more complex to measure and constitute more of a moving target. As such they are less easily integrated into this approach. A more controversial view is that career as an orderly sequence of choosing is a myth and that empirical evidence[6] suggests that people are:

> pulled by opportunities and images of the future, pushed by reactions to the past and the demands of the present; and all the time buffetted by the uncertainty surrounding these changes and forces.

The myth of a planned career is encouraged by those in positions of influence in education, recruitment specialists and managers themselves. In reality:

> directed choice in careers can only be exercised by managers seizing and exploiting the unpredicted moments of change and opportunity.

Even if a manager's career does not appear to have an underlying consistency, the theories and concepts embodied in the matching and process models are useful as diagnostic tools. The senior manager may find one that relates more closely than others to a subordinate's behaviour. This can then serve as a focus for discussion of possible career transitions.

7.4 Motivational patterns

Motivation is a crucial concept in understanding careers and is important to organizations as it is a source of competitive advantage to have a committed and flexible work-force. 'Commitment' here is the attraction to and identification with the goals and values of the organization.

When a job choice has been made, what then encourages the manager to stay and make a career with the organization? The answer is the extent to which the employer offers rewards consistent with the person's motivation. It has been defined[7] as 'the direction and persistence of action' and contains the idea of:

> a driving force within individuals by which they attempt to achieve some goal to satisfy some need or expectation.

It is also cyclical in that achieving a goal (such as promotion) to satisfy a need (for status and money) can generate an even stronger need (for *more* status and money) – a fact long recognized by market researchers and advertisers. A three-fold classification[8] of the motivation to work, built on past theories of psychologists such as Herzberg and Maslow, is that of:

- *economic rewards*: pay, benefits, goods, which are all instrumental
- *intrinsic satisfaction*: nature of the work itself, interest, personal growth and development
- *social relationships*.

Motivation, job satisfaction and performance depend on the strength of peoples' needs and expectations and the extent to which they are fulfilled. If these are blocked, for example, by the non-fulfilment of an expectation of promotion, it can lead to them exhibiting problem-solving behaviour to get around the cause of the blockage – in this case, perhaps seeing the boss and finding out why. Alternatively, it can lead to various reactions (physical and verbal aggression against individuals or the organization) so they become extremely disruptive. People may also become fixated, carry on doing the same things without insight and, maybe, finally withdraw. This kind of behaviour leads to plateauing, early retirement or exit and can lower morale if not checked early enough.

Many different theories of motivation exist that are well summarized elsewhere.[9] Their presentation would cause a different emphasis to be given to career planning than that which is required here. It is sufficient to say that they can be broadly grouped into content and process theories.

The content theories

The content theories, with protagonists such as Maslow, Alderfer, Herzberg and McClelland, focus on understanding individuals' needs, their relative strengths and particular goals. The types of problem situations at work to which these might be applied are, for example, what particular combination of compensation and benefits, flexibility of contractual conditions, working environment and prospects will be suitable for one manager and not another? Why are some managers motivated to satisfy needs for achievement and power while others seek instead satisfying relationships at work? These types of theory provide a starting point and a systematic understanding for unravelling the interplay of the various elements at work.

The process theories

The process theories, devised by such people as Vroom and Porter and Lawler, attempt to explain how certain variables interact to produce behaviour.

EXPECTANCY THEORIES

These propound that, if, for example, there is a strong need for advancement and an expectation that *who* you know is more important than *what* you know or how you perform at work, then certain behaviours will follow. Efforts and energy will be expended on cultivating contacts and being visible rather than becoming an expert or working too hard.

The key element here is the assessment (correct or possibly incorrect) of probabilities that certain types of effort will lead to the achievement of certain types of performance and the satisfaction of particular goals. These, in turn, are likely to lead to rewards, and the amount of effort expended will be related to the value of the reward itself. The individual strength of these different variables (effort, reward, value) determines the level of motivation. That is where the individual's personal knowledge and skills come into play in correctly identifying and assessing these variables and the relationship between them. These themes help to explain why, in some cases, there is no direct relation between an individual identifying an internal need and being able to satisfy it. Perceptual differences and misunderstandings about the variables and their interrelationship can spoil the chances of success.

All this also indicates to managers the importance of establishing for themselves a clear link between the effort and standards of performance required, and the personal value of the reward, which are under their control. It also underlines for general managers the importance of recognizing that there may be other external complicating factors that can reduce motivation. This is the philosophy underlying performance management and performance-related pay looked at in Chapter 6. In career terms, the amount of effort expected (commitment, competence and personal mobility) must be seen by the individual to lead to satisfying the organizations' particular demands and that it will be rewarded.

EQUITY THEORIES

A refinement of how the attractiveness of rewards are perceived is provided by another group of process theories – the equity theories of motivation.

Take two people who are promoted at the same time, but one after three years and the other after only one year with the company. The longer server, who may have initially been happy with the news and spurred to greater efforts, may suddenly feel demotivated on hearing the news about the colleague. The latter has received the same degree of recognition for a perceived reduced amount of effort.

Certain behaviours from both parties may then follow, to which their manager can be alerted. The slower achiever may reduce the amount of effort normally applied to the job. He or she may belittle the success of the high achiever, putting it down to luck, an easier set of tasks, a more favourable climate in the organization and so on. He or she may then engage in overly competitive behaviour for the next promotion. The current position now appears devalued because of the 'excessive' amount of work required to achieve it. In extreme cases, the individual may physically or psychologically withdraw from the competition. The fast achiever may, in turn, devalue the colleagues' contribution or even seek to eliminate him or her altogether from being a possible candidate for the next promotion.

GOAL THEORY

Another process theory[10] emphasizes the existence of goals in focusing people's efforts and that these are based on an individuals' values and wants. The motivating force of goals depends on their difficulty, the willingness to expend energy and effort to attain them and the amount of feedback given about performance.

As far as careers are concerned, this shows the importance of consultation about any objectives that may be set by and for managers and the organizational expectations associated with them. The perceived ease (or difficulty of meeting them) could be a real stumbling block in their achievement, even if they are within the managers' capabilities. The difficulty level may also be determined by where the perceived locus of control in the means to their attainment lies: within the individual (effort and ability) or outside (uncontrollable factors or luck).

The known motivation of goal-setting behaviour is also crucial as it prevents drift in careers, especially where people may not know or care where they are going. The techniques of self-assessment referred to later in this chapter focus in one way or another on goal setting and these related issues, concluding in an action plan.

What we can learn from the theories

The proliferation of all these theories indicates what a complex and difficult area motivation is. What this mix offers is different ways for the general manager to tackle the demotivated manager. They provide specific aspects to focus on in relation to careers: goals, expectations, rewards, effort, probabilities of success and the ways in which these all interact.

Studies

A study [11] that examined the relationship between effort and reward among over 300 male managers in 6 large UK-based organizations concluded that, while managers felt that they were having to make greater efforts in their jobs, the rewards were seen to be declining. Consequently, 'their commitment to their jobs and careers are diminishing' and satisfactions were being sought outside their working life. They believed that 'opportunities for personal growth and development' were very limited. This was unacceptable to them, as the content theories of motivation would have predicted.

Compared to their own situation, they saw the independent professionals as being well ahead in the earnings and satisfaction league. The authors speculated that this was because the latter group were not seen to have the career blockages of the former. They could also see a direct relationship between effort and reward when their clients paid them, a contributing factor to their satisfaction, which is what the expectancy theories would predict.

For the managers, the effort-reward link was continuously monitored and evaluated. While accepting the need for being results-oriented, they were 'unhappy with the measures used'. The authors concluded that a more instrumental attitude to work was arising as only 35 per cent of the group disagreed that 'the personal costs of career outweigh the benefits'.

This general view was supported by the percentages endorsing other statements measuring similar orientations. The most important major sources of satisfaction were family relationships, 57 per cent, compared with career achievements, 18 per cent, and present job, 12 per cent, indicating a shift away from the idea of always putting work first.

Another study of managers[12] also pointed to the cost of managerial success. Only 25 per cent of the managers saw the weekends as a time to relax and pursue their own interests. The rest saw it as a means of building up their energy for the coming week. Some 45 per cent were dissatisfied with their distribution of time and energy. The damage to family life was not so much the number of hours worked but the inability of managers to 'switch off'.

Individuals only have a certain amount of energy to invest. If work is all-consuming, the family suffers; if work is boring or unfulfilling managers start their own businesses, clockwatch or take every opportunity to follow their leisure interests. They develop an 'avocation' and put just enough energy into their work to keep employed. John, aged 35, was one such character.

Married but without children, he was in a central research and advisory role and was consulted by other parts of the organization. He liked the intellectual aspects of the work, but did not wish to transfer into a line position to gain promotion. His wife had her own export business and they planned to settle in another European country. There he intended to write up his last 12 years' occupational experiences and follow an academic and journalistic career.

Such an example illustrates that motivation at work is therefore not only complicated in itself but must also be considered in relation to a person's overall motivation in non-work life. General managers need to take an interest in the *whole* person before they can begin to understand the context of career motivation and certainly long before they can hope to influence it.

7.5 Career themes

Motivations in accepting and working in jobs and following careers may not always be apparent, either to managers themselves or their bosses. Sometimes, unbeknown to individuals, there may be a link that emerges. As we have seen in Chapter 3, transitions between jobs involve some degree of uncertainty and even crisis. Once these have been resolved, a person finds the appropriate behaviour and attitudes to adopt. Each transition yields some self-knowledge about likes and dislikes in a job, strengths and weaknesses and needs and wants.

Career anchors

Over the years this builds into an orientation to work, a career anchor.[13]

THE COMPONENTS

Each career anchor has three components:

- talents and abilities
- motives and needs
- attitudes and values.

These elements all interact with each other, people tending to want and value those things they are good at. If a person takes a job where these attributes are not felt to be in harmony, it is said that they will be pulled back to doing something that is more consistent with them. In other words, their career is 'anchored' by certain factors.

ANCHORING FACTORS

The anchoring factors are:

- *managerial*: the aim is to remain in control of events while dealing with risks, incomplete information and difficulties so interpersonal skills, analytical ability and handling emotional and interpersonal crises are vital for success
- *technical/functional*: the self-image is one of competence in a specialist

field, therefore, intrinsic motivation is the key and the individual will resist being promoted out of the specialism, fearing and disliking general management as a job
- *security*: the person wishes the organization to look after him or her and accepts their definition of career, thus avoiding the uncertainty of leaving, so needs and talents may pass unrecognized; if the employee has both managerial and technical competence, the drive for security may prevent aspirations to a position in the higher echelons where emotional stability has to be maintained amid uncertainty and, equally, the individual may keep changing organizations for a similar job to keep secure rather than hold different jobs in the same organization
- *creativity*: a need to invent or create a new product or service that can be personally attributed to the individual – this may overlap with a need for autonomy
- *autonomy*: a need for independence when the organization is found to be too restrictive or intrusive into their private lives – these individuals will also want to set their own lifestyles.

THE FUNCTIONS OF CAREER ANCHORS

These are many. They help to organize experiences and make sense of what has happened by identifying the threads that may run through various career moves. They may also provide clues if job choices do not work out, as well as guiding a person when he or she has to choose between two apparently similar jobs. They also produce stability as, in a crisis, people tend to revert to what they know. This does not mean that these anchors restrict growth; rather, they determine the base point from which it can happen and from which choices can be made. They enable people to answer the questions:

- 'What do I want to be?'
- 'What job should I be doing?'
- 'What values must I not compromise on?'

Most important of all, they are self-defined standards for judging the success of the internal career. As such, they are useful for thinking about new careeer directions because they help in understanding past decisions, experiences and mistakes.

An alternative group of classifications

Another empirical classification of career themes[14] is that of getting:

– ahead
– secure
– free
– high
– balanced.

There is some overlap with the previous classification in the getting secure, getting free (or, autonomy) and getting high (or, technical competence) aspects, but the rest are different.

THE GETTING AHEAD TYPE

For this type who aims for the top of the hierarchy and likes status and power, there are certain strategies for success. Here the internal and external careers coincide so, first and foremost, it is important to know the organization thoroughly, find a sponsor and make the job the first priority. It is necessary to make sure that the right experience is obtained, visible assignments are undertaken and opportunities are seized.

If this is achieved, the personal benefits are comfort, convenience and the luxuries that money can buy. The costs are the constant striving, health problems, personal relationships and persistent drive for self-development.

Those with this orientation are said to be easy to control as they are self-motivated and manage themselves in accordance with their goals, which will be the internalized goals of the company. They are likely to have good management of people, organizational and analytical problem-solving skills as they have to diagnose the organization to determine their own role and value inside it.

Julian was one such getting ahead type. Although he had left school without any formal educational qualifications, he had a keen mind and was willing to learn. This brought him rapid promotion until he was deputy of a large professional department. Nothing stood in his way (he had no dependants and he was financially secure) and he had all the trappings of success (a fast car, went on foreign holidays, owned two homes and had income from a property he rented out). His thrusting style and abrasiveness had so far served him well, but he now is sensitive enough to realize that to get the top job he will have to have good team-building skills and must dilute the aggression. The energy and drive are all there to make him successful, but only if they are channelled towards the success of the team.

THE GETTING SECURE TYPE

This type seeks permanent employment, wanting stability, routines and predictability. Security is an end in itself, a more comfortable state than any other. In return for an anxiety-free and secure existence with recognition, the employee offers loyalty and dedication to the job and organization.

Such individuals can be able, but do not thrive on competition like the getting ahead type. They tend to form the middle management ranks. Their problem is image. No one readily admits to wanting security, yet these types are often the solid citizens the organization wants and holders of the organization culture.

Their strategy for success here is to find the company who needs their dedication. Like the getting ahead type, these people have to correctly read the organizational culture, conform to the norms and become a safe pair of hands. However, their unquestioning loyalty may be seen by some as lacking in personal principles sacrificing being true to themselves.

The benefits for this type are clearly less stress and strain but the costs are that, over time, they find it difficult to survive without the company. Sudden changes or a new top management team may leave them feeling very exposed as they then have no stable reference point for how to behave.

Managing them needs appreciation and a belief in order, with clear rules and rewards. An example of this type was Edward who was head of a strategically-minded IT function in the financial services sector. He was so keen not to rock the boat that he would often miss stating a point of view that would have been of value to his superiors. His security-mindedness spilled over into his private life. He could retire comfortably at 45 if he so chose. Security was often gained at the expense of making friends as he saw interpersonal relations as a risky area. He therefore had few confidants and did not relate easily to new colleagues.

THE GETTING FREE TYPE

These also need to choose their organizations carefully but for different reasons. They value independence in getting their work done *when* they want and *how* they want.

Consultants, hi-tech specialists and medical and legal experts are examples of this type and need an environment that will tolerate these needs. They nevertheless have to perform to the required standard and pay their dues to the organization to stay employed. They need to make sure that they are visible enough when they do appear and be real experts to be valued.

Managing this type can be difficult as others at a similar level can resent their success and feel that they are not pulling their weight, but the getting-free types have their highly-placed sponsors and always come through when the chips are down. They require firm deadlines, budgets and an indication of what is not permitted as well as not too much interpersonal dependence in their job. The benefits of this mode of operation are job satisfaction and the ability to grow and develop. The costs are likely to be workaholicism, loneliness and the toll of always having to acquire new expertise to stay ahead of the game. They can be isolated and involved in struggles to defend their organizational patch.

Mike was well-qualified as an architect and not inclined to seek out social relations at work. He had held several lecturing posts but decided that this was becoming too much of a tie because of the large increases in student numbers. He left for a series of jobs in a local community planning department, but found the routines and hours constraining and moved to the leisure field. Because he was creative, entrepreneurial and able, he had become too valuable to his boss and needed to break out again. The ideal combination for him was to secure a part-time lectureship at an educational establishment and undertake freelance work in a small, niche consultancy.

THE GETTING HIGH TYPE

Seeking intrinsic satisfaction from work, deriving their identity from being extremely competent and able in acquiring new ideas concepts and techniques, these types have to obtain exciting work through their ability to produce high-quality work and communicate effectively with their superiors. Some of them have a low boredom threshold and may neglect the routine but necessary procedures for operating in an organization. In the pursuit of stimulation, social relationships may be neglected that, if cultivated, could generate the exciting work they desire. They may be seen as disloyal and not team players as they spiral in and out of jobs to avoid any boring patches.

The benefits of being this type are the job satisfaction and personal development. The costs are that they can be seen as loners, unwilling to work in a team and difficult to manage. Therefore at work they are not seen as a long-term investment. The restlessness may spill over into family life, with these types finding permanent relationships constraining.

Managing these people requires that they are not allowed to invest too much effort and resources in attention to detail at the expense of overall organization objectives. The 'best' is the enemy of the good here, as they tend not to see 'the big picture' while they focus on feeding their need for challenge. They thrive on interesting assignments that are not 'quick and dirty' and driven by contingencies. They are valuable to the organization needing state-of-the-art work and excellent technical competence. To make the best use of their skills and give them attention and recognition, they need sponsors to champion their work and sell their skills to other parts of the organization and to protect their position.

James was a getting high type. He was a telecommunications expert, single and committed to being at the leading edge of his subject. He made a decision to leave his electronics company and join a consultancy that he thought would provide continuous variety. The first few assignments did just that. Then the requests began to be of a more routine nature and his manager insisted that he took them to keep his utilization on fee-earning work high. This in turn led to his resignation until a director found him a position as consultant to his colleagues and to the international firm. This allowed him to keep his knowledge up to date and have the variety of short, chargeable inputs on many different leading edge projects.

THE GETTING BALANCED TYPE

For these individuals satisfaction and motivation is juggling career, self-development and personal relationships. Each aspect is important but seen as not being worth sacrificing for the other. The balance can be achieved concurrently or sequentially, with one element being dominant, followed by the other two. The latter situation fits the dual career family (see Chapter 3) well, where individuals may have to put personal development on hold while the spouse changes career or where both have to refuse promotion temporarily for the sake of a young family.

Satisfying the getting balanced type depends on finding a suitable organization. This is one that values having balanced types and does not expect a 16-hour day from all its staff, disallowing the existence of a private life. A clue to this will be the presence of some of the policies outlined in Chapter 6.

Employing this type of person needs flexibility on both sides. Individuals must prove their worth to the organization before it will be flexible in its approach to their careers. This can involve, on occasions, working long hours or handling crises at a personal cost to show loyalty and demonstrate that one is serious about the job. If the organization responds, then these people can be good performers because they appreciate they have the best combination of their career and personal world. The balancing act can be very fine. If an employer believes that at a critical time the extra effort will not be produced, then their value to the organization will be reduced.

The benefits of this getting balanced approach are contented and committed staff. The difficulty is that their time and energy is measured so they may not have the ability to foster close working relationships with their boss or colleagues by socializing outside work.

Managing these managers requires a clarity of what the limits to flexibility are, the ability to negotiate and an understanding of the individuals' circumstances. These people tend to hide this orientation and portray a getting ahead one instead. They do this to avoid the misinterpretations that can arise about their lack of visible dedication and minimal socializing at work. Their work-directed energies may come in bursts just as their personally focused efforts may do the same to cope with a crisis and this needs some understanding on the part of their bosses.

James was a getting balanced type. With three teenage children and a wife teaching in a special school, he held a secure engineering job with a large service industry. Determined not to disrupt the family situation, he drove 180 miles to and from work each day. He had developed accounting and financial skills along the way and was in line for promotion. This he knew would take him away from his present domestic location. He has not discussed this with his wife nor does he feel able to tell his boss for fear of ending his career. The balancing act is getting precarious as he knows the organization wants him to move to unblock the career path for a younger man. He has decided that he needs to do some life-goal planning with his wife to see where the balance needs to be shifted (if only temporarily) before he speaks to his boss.

SUMMARY

An advantage of this categorization of career themes is that the definition of career success is internally generated. If the type can be correctly identified, then many other behaviours follow. General managers are likely to meet many of the types and may find some of them in conflict with their own orientations. However, if they focus on the benefits associated with each type and manage them in different ways, they may still find it possible to encourage a company culture that allows this diversity (and therefore flexibility) to coexist.

7.6 Career and personality

Underlying the notion of career themes is the managers' own personality. Two questions that are frequently asked about career and personality are whether certain types of personality enter particular fields and whether time spent in an occupation produces a certain type of individual. The answer is certainly 'yes' to both questions, as our everyday experience tells us. Rather than attempt to give a detailed elaboration of this answer here, it is more fruitful to consider certain dimensions[14] that are related to peoples' presenting behaviour, attitudes, motivations and choices within certain occupational groups. These are

- *stereotypes*: occupations present certain images – the bookish lawyer, the practical engineer, the creative advertising manager, the dynamic salesman, the painstaking accountant
- *common skills and aptitudes*: certain occupations require minimum intellectual levels, call on stamina and so on
- *anticipatory socialization*: before entry to an occupation or status position, individuals learn how to behave in accordance with certain roles and certain values are imparted – the research chemist has strong ethics about accurate reporting, the marketing manager will place a premium on sound analysis and presentation, the doctor will be non-judgemental
- *common interests*: members of an occupational group will share common interests, say, in the practising of skills, status, appearance and expectations of remuneration
- *common language*: occupational jargon arises as a shorthand and a very specific means of communication between members
- *shared ideologies*: a belief in a common purpose, shared values, internal grading and disciplinary system and style of presentation
- *shared preoccupations*: common concerns, ethical or technical, for instance.

The degree of identity between an individual and an occupation will depend on the extent to which the requirements of that occupation are consistent with that person's self-image. The closer the two, the more stereotyped that occupational personality will seem.

Cognitive styles

At a more specific level, there are aspects of personality, such as introversion and extroversion, that are now part of common language and used by recruitment specialists. Less well known is the term 'cognitive style'. In one review of the area [16] it is defined as:

> The distinct and consistent strategies people show in their approach to information and problem solving.

IMBALANCES IN INTELLECTUAL RESPONSES

An extreme style is said to reflect:

an imbalance in intellectual responses that makes it particularly well suited to jobs that similarly involve specialized information, analysis and communication.

DETAILS FIRST OR THE GENERAL POINTS FIRST

There are many different ways of considering style. Some individuals build from details up to the 'big picture', others start with a broad brush and fill in the details later. Certain styles may develop from continuous exposure to particular kinds of information and problems. Lawyers, for example, are very verbal in their presentation of facts, as are Civil Servants. The use of diagrams and flip charts to explore and explain problems is not their natural first choice of medium. By contrast, this would be the choice of visualizers – who tend to be scientists and technologists – or those who think in systems terms.

CONVERGENT AND DIVERGENT THINKING

Another distinction[17] is that of the convergent thinker – one who is logical, deductive, analytical, one answer – and the divergent thinker – one who is inductive, intuitive, creative, gives many answers. The former tends to be associated with the hard sciences and the latter with the arts and humanities. The section devoted to the management of specialists raised the question of whether they can become general managers. It is not just a question of training and exposure, although these are important, it also depends on how extreme their cognitive style is. Specialists are valuable precisely because of their extreme styles: auditors for their precision and caution; lawyers for their verbal accuracy and dexterity.

FIELD DEPENDENCE AND FIELD INDEPENDENCE

Field dependence[18] refers to the extent to which an individual relies on the context surrounding problem-solving behaviour.

In contrast, field-independence is the degree to which the problem and its solution can be isolated from the surrounding information and constraints. Possessors of the latter style tend to rely on their own perceptions and act with autonomy. They prefer non-social situations and some physical and psychological distance between themselves and others. They do not feel any need to 'follow the herd' when making decisions. They tend to be more interested in concepts rather than people and their strengths are for data analysis and independent review.

The field dependents in contrast, rely on external factors in problem solving and, in the process, pay more attention to social cues. They enjoy social situations and are likely to be physically and emotionally close to others. They are likely to be more interested in people rather than concepts. Their strengths are in understanding people and seeing relationships between apparently separate problems. They are drawn to follow careers in sales, counselling and teaching.

The field independents tend to follow occupations in the hard sciences and engineering fields. However, these are broad generalizations and there are similar divisions within specialisms within occupations.

The implications here for managing people and careers are that the strongly field independent will want to maintain distance from the 'groupiness' of the corporate culture in contrast to the field dependents. They will probably be indifferent to the induction and socialization processes (see Chapter 5) and resist attempts at what they would see as being indoctrinated.

PRECEPTIVE AND RECEPTIVE APPROACHES

This style is a strategy for information gathering.[19]

The preceptive individuals filter data and do this by looking for patterns and deviations from their expectations, scanning the world around them quickly.

Receptive people respond to the data stimulus itself, focusing on detail. Their careful reasoning is unlikely to overlook relevant facts. The preceptive is more able to organize large amounts of disparate data whereas the receptive would be overwhelmed by it. The latter style demands attention to all the pieces of data and there is no easy way to reduce the conceptual load.

These behaviours are likely to be reinforced by a particular value system that each regards as the right way to test out the real world. Therefore, those with strong tendencies in either direction would feel uncomfortable with the others' style.

Marketing managers are supposed to be strong preceptors, sensing their market, spotting the beginnings of trends and drawing patterns from all the disparate information of sales reports. These people will thrive on jobs involving filtering and sensing.

On the other hand, careers well suited to the receptor are those of computer programmer, engineer, auditor, production manager or architect, where there is an opportunity to display professionalism and skill through attention to detail.

SYSTEMATIC AND INTUITIVE STYLE THINKING

The systematic or methodological thinker defines how the problem will be approached, the surrounding constraints and the plan of attack. These people are aware of all the key steps and proceed in an orderly way, searching and analysing, as 'the methodology guarantees the solution'.

The intuitive thinker may look over a range of ideas and information before even defining the problem, resolving some contradictions in the data along the way. Then, this type checks whether each step relates to the whole picture to see if it fits. Once a broad feel is obtained, lines of enquiry are rejected and options reduced.

It is important for senior managers to recognize that the intuitive thinker does not verbalize the problem-solving process to the same degree as the systematic does and so may even appear illogical or disorganized. There may be false starts but the process can be brought to a successful conclusion.

When they allocate work, senior managers need to realize that systematic thinkers have a preference for clear-cut problems, while intuitive thinkers prefer problems that are open-ended and have no right answer. Systematic and intuitive thinkers would have difficulty working closely together as the intuitive approach would be regarded as messy or badly thought out by the systematic thinker and the systematic thinker would be seen as rigid, uncreative and lacking in vision by the intuitive thinker.

Putting these styles together with the previous ones, a systematic receptive person would be likely to be an engineer or a programmer, and an intuitive preceptive person might be an advertising executive. A receptive intuitive person could be a field sales manager and a systematic preceptive person might be a systems analyst.

Misfits

Career and personality may not match for reasons apart from cognitive style.[19] A competence misfit may be someone who transfers from sales to marketing but does not have the skills; or an employee who performs well but has no confidence.

Second, there may be an enjoyment misfit who is extremely competent but derives no enjoyment from work, such as managers of people with an excessive amount of paperwork or managers who would prefer to do a specialist job.

Third, an individual may be a moral misfit. Someone may find the selling methods of a company abhorrent or, alternatively, use bribery and undue string-pulling to gain an edge over rivals in what should be a team-based operation.

Each misfit problem may severely affect an employee's personal as well as working life as the discomfort has to be endured for at least eight hours daily at work.

Types of manager

Another way of looking at the relationship between career, personality and work-adjustment is the match between the individual and organizational values.[21] From a survey of 250 male managers in 12 major companies in the USA, 4 types of manager were identified. Each style had its own characteristics and consequences for those around them:

- *the jungle fighter*: the goal is power as life is seen as a jungle where the fittest survive – peers are accomplices or enemies and subordinates are to be dominated or they will get the upper hand – so careerwise, this type makes many enemies, a fact that can damage further chances of success
- *the company man*: the goal is conservation and this type of manager tries to enhance the corporate integrity and minimize differences so the atmosphere is one of discipline and service and, as this person is so obsessed with politics, the aim is to protect one's own career, never lead or innovate
- *the gamesman*: the goal is to be a winner and a star so subordinates are only considered if they contribute to the team's success (if not they will be discarded dispassionately when appropriate) and this manager is a collection of paradoxes – playful yet driven, a team player yet needing stardom – life is a game but the gamesman may be branded as too flippant and immature for a career in top management
- *the craftsman*: the goal is autonomy and opportunities for interesting work so the concerns for quality, perfectionism and self-containment prevent the emergence of any leadership, meaning that this manager is not interested in cooperating to achieve something larger than that attainable simply through his or her own efforts.

These four organizational personality types would fit comfortably with the types of culture (respectively power, role, task and person) outlined in Chapter 5. These cultures are, in turn, conditioned by their organizational structures.

Conclusion

There is no doubt that personality is an important general concept, but to be of practical use, its role in career has to be determined through specific research, not what merely appears to be valid on the face of it, such as the stereotype of the extrovert salesman.

7.7 Self-assessment and development techniques

There are many techniques for self-assessment and development that can be used in a variety of combinations. The overall purpose of these is to help people gain more control over their lives and, in the process, they may discover dormant abilities, interests and motivation. All this provides the information on which to base the setting of goals, making decisions and producing personal career plans. The career plans need to be set in such a way as to convey a sense of direction, but not be seen as confining.

Self-assessment techniques

The methods used have similarities with those used in development and assessment centres, although their purposes are different, as is the way in which the results are used. The emphasis here is much more personal and may be carried out in conjunction with counselling. Some of the methods used are:

– structured activities, such as workbooks
– discussion
– individual self-analysis
– group work, for example decision making and problem solving
– questionnaires
– personality inventories
– role plays
– in-tray exercises.

They are all designed to provide information about oneself, using any other relevant sources, say, from appraisal, assessment and development centres. They are intended to help to answer such questions as:

– 'Where am I now?'
– 'How did I get here?'
– 'Where am I going?'
– 'How do I get there?'

No individual technique is infallible. Taken together, pieces of feedback and themes will emerge that can then be discussed with others to see if there is some consistency.

The sequencing of these self-assessment techniques tends to follow a broad pattern:

- reviewing the past
- assessing the current situation
- imagining the future and goal setting
- action plans.

LIFE LINES TECHNIQUE

When reviewing the past, individuals may be asked to write a short autobiography, picking out certain episodes, learning points, feelings about their situation or particular influences in their lives.

They may use a technique called 'life lines'. This requires them to define success in their own terms and then plot peaks and troughs (high and low levels of success, respectively) at five-year intervals, say from the age of 15 to the present. On asking themselves why these occurred, how long they lasted and how they felt about them, themes may be identified (for instance, a search for novelty, a breaking of relationships and so on).

A CAREER REVIEW

Another technique would be to do a career review, listing various features under the following headings:

Date	Job	Likes	Dislikes	Did well	Did badly

Underneath each heading, the relevant facts are entered and later analysed by the individual alone or with another person.

CVS

They might also do a conventional CV in more detail that highlights specific achievements. Career anchors and orientations are of particular interest here, as are feelings about and interpretations of the transition process (Chapter 3) between various jobs. These help to identify the links between the jobs and the learning that occurred.

SKILLS AUDITS

Next, the current situation would be probed with techniques such as a skills audit (showing strengths and weaknesses) and questionnaires about values (family, social, political, religious, aesthetic and so on). These together indicate what is believed to be important in a person's life. The importance of these overall values may not be seen by individuals until they are called upon to write them down.

One person, called Peter, who had been half-heartedly applying for jobs because he was desperately unhappy at work, only came to realize why when he had listed his three most important values. These were a challenging job, money for leisure interests and security. A colleague pointed out that to want challenge *and* security at the same time was probably incompatible. Also, a challenging job might not leave as much time for leisure pursuits. He therefore agreed to rethink his values.

After this clarification, there is the option to examine aptitudes and potential, unused abilities and overall concerns about the general situation.

PERSONALITY AND INTEREST INVENTORIES

Personality and interest may be used, for example, to gain information about one's tolerance of ambiguity, attitudes to risk, ability to adapt – all may provide information about what kind of opportunities and constraints exist for an individual.

Some organizations deliberately leave boundaries between functions unclear so that initiatives may appear and one will eventually establish itself. An individual with a low tolerance of ambiguity may be very uncomfortable here. Motivation and work interests are also of particular significance here. These can be tapped by asking individuals to choose what is important to them in a job now or asking them to compare a job they liked with one they hated. There are a number of other areas that can be covered, such as the way individuals handle life changes and transitions, their health situation, financial and other resources and their relationships. Non-work aspects can also be explored such as leisure, family, social activities and geography to see what motivators and inhibitors there may be on career plans.

OTHER EXERCISES

Focusing more on the future and goals, individuals may be asked about their ideal job, ignoring any constraints. Other well-known tasks are the 'million dollar', the 'brain tumour' and the 'write your own obituary' exercises. These techniques are designed to encourage free thinking:

- 'If I had a million dollars I would . . .'
- 'If I only had six months to live I would like to achieve the following . . .'
- 'John Smith (you) died yesterday. He had led a full and active life . . .'

Out of these exercises come the ideal situation, what a person is really striving for, personal goals and development needs. These can be tested against an individual's own thinking ('What would be the consequences if I succeed or fail?') and with others who might be directly affected ('How would that affect my partner's career?') or with people who could help in some way ('Why should they help me achieve that?') Opportunities and options can then be listed with the likelihood of success, things that need to be in place and the resources that need to be acquired.

Development

SMART

The action plan has to be developed to attain the goals. Sub-objectives have to be formulated that are SMART, that is:

- Specific
- Measurable
- Agreed
- Realistic
- Timebound and Trackable.

While not pretending that all this is easy, difficulties encountered in the SMART process may enable a rethinking or refocusing of career goals that can be helpful. Using this formula and having discussed the ideas with the boss, a manager might say:

> I want to receive two promotions in the next three-and-a-half years, the second out of my specialist area.

It also helps if there are milestones along the way to monitor and assess progress and identify possible helps and hindrances. Resources or skills may or may not be available to achieve objectives and if this can be highlighted early on, remedial action can be taken to obtain them. If James knows he needs an MBA to be considered for a job in two years' time, then he can go about acquiring it, having set out his objectives and laid out a broad plan.

Where some of these objectives involve change, inventories can be completed by the individual on what and how to change. For instance, 'To be more effective, I need to . . .' and the manager can select from a substantial list of activities or attributes those that apply, and the extent to which they do so. This helps to flesh out the main plan and pinpoint areas where and when help may be needed.

Are all these techniques accurate?

First, there is no reason to actively deceive oneself. If the self-perception is inaccurate, this will be obvious when the manager discusses the results with someone else.

Second, the use of multiple sources and techniques builds in a high degree of redundant information that is more resistant to distortion. This can highlight contradictions and inconsistencies as well as reinforce themes and make the whole process more reliable. Information is progressively sifted and can be tested against the opinion of others or a trained counsellor to aid self-exploration and analysis. General managers can assist by identifying opportunities and rewarding efforts at self-development by adding new responsibilities or asking managers to coordinate special interest groups.

Some of the key lessons learned from a study of methods used by the General Electric Company[22] may be summarized as follows:

- the role of line managers is to set an example to their staff by first understanding their own career, otherwise staff will not see that properly executed career planning is beneficial
- the experience of career planning is necessary to be an effective helper
- managers are less likely to feel uncomfortable in this helping role when they have a known and agreed method of assisting
- individuals need to progress in small steps to digest the information provided about them
- managers should say what they have agreed to do for their staff.

The eagerness with which managers usually seek out relevant literature on these techniques and the anecdotal evidence suggest that they find self-assessment techniques very valuable in clarifying their thinking on careers. In many cases they come as a revelation and the fact that their output can be reflected upon and talked through with others at a chosen time is a bonus. In some cases, as the next section will show, the questioning and self-discovery process has been systematized in a comprehensive yet flexible way.

7.8 Computerized tools for self-development

Databases

With the advance of computerized systems and communicating networks, there are now available databases of self-assessment techniques and occupational information. The former (personality inventories, occupational values and interest questionnaires) are increasingly becoming accessible to individuals on diskette, with automatically printed profiles and interpretation of scores. Alternatively, these can be completed and returned to agents or suppliers for machine processing and interpretation. In some cases, recruiters are using them and feeding back the profiles (compared with particular occupational groups) to individual applicants.

It should be made clear that these mechanically based profiles have a limited value. They are good for comparing individual scores with those of others in, say, similar job categories or backgrounds, but they still need talking through with a third party. This is because there will inevitably be some questions about the conclusions, the force with which they may be expected to apply and the particular conditions that may enhance or even negate them. Reports of 'low capacity to change' or 'low growth potential' (often gleaned from preferences rather than actual behaviour) may appear entirely incorrect when an individual is faced with a real-life situation.

There are also various databases of jobs, opportunities and training that are offered and maintained by different organizations. MICRODOORS (Data on Occupational Retrieval Systems) is run by the Manpower Services Commission and has information on some 800 occupations. This enables occupational matching to be carried out against a list of variable criteria such as interest, abilities and so on. ECCTIS 2000 (Educational Counselling and Credit Transfer Information Service) operates the UK information system of courses in higher and further education for the Department of Education and Science. The service is delivered through contracts with organizations, including British Telecom, The Council for National Academic Awards (CNAA), The Careers Research and Advisory Service (CRAC) and the Open University, to name but a few. ROGET (the Register of Graduate Employment and Training) is a compendium of employers of graduates and available jobs. Another, called GRAD-SCOPE, is a database and computer search system to help graduates locate information on occupations and employers

One very sophisticated system is that of SIGI Plus (System of Interactive Guidance and Information), developed by the Educational Testing Service, Princeton in the USA. It consists of nine modules that combine self-assessment, information about different kinds of occupations, preparation methods for entry, decision-making skills and career plan implementation. In the information section, it allows the service provider to add local information so that it appears more tailored.

Another system, developed in the UK, is called PROSPECT.* This is a state-of-the-art, computer-assisted, careers guidance system with over 20 modules. They can be used in any sequence and are based on four key stages in the decision-making process.

The first stage involves the user in self-assessment of values, interests, abilities and skills, including psychometric tests. This diagnostic profile can then be stored for subsequent use.

Stage two centres on the identification of career options available to the individual. A database of occupations can be searched according to at least 100 criteria, either singly or in combination, to find suitable occupations.

Stage three employs decision aids, so that the preferences for certain occupations can be compared with the individuals' chances of success in entering them. This results in the indication of a 'best option'.

The final stage is focused on how to develop a career plan based on this 'best option'. This plan includes advice on finding job information, making applications and preparing CVs. Further refinements are still being developed.

Two key strengths of the system are that it is suitable for exploratory purposes and it is very flexibile – both crucial features in career development.

7.9 Conclusion

While these assessment and development techniques can be used by individuals on their own, assistance from the organization and the general manager in 'reality testing' can be of enormous help to staff. If senior managers have a broader appreciation of some of the areas covered in this chapter, they are likely to be better boards for their own managers and encourage them to help themselves. Wrongly placed and demotivated individuals cost money and are a bad influence on those around them. The senior general manager has the knowledge and ability to acquire help to prevent this.

Action questions

SENIOR MANAGERS

What resources might it be possible to commit to helping your managers to explore their own careers?

* The author is indebted to Peter Pierce-Price, Adviser to the PROSPECT consortium, funded by the DES, Corporation of the City of London, BP and ICI, for details of the system briefly summarized here. Any omissions are my own.

What would you need to do to justify this?

MANAGERS

Are you using as many opportunities as possible to gain self-insight?
Are you aware of your own motivations and career pattern to date?

HUMAN RESOURCE SPECIALISTS

Do you put aside enough time to deal with career issues?
Do you feel comfortable with current concepts, tools and techniques to
deal with career development?

References

1. Evans, P., and F. Bartolomé, *Must Success Cost So Much?*, Grant McIntyre, 1980.
2. Evans, P., and F. Bartolomé, op. cit.
3. Dalton, G., P. Thompson and R. Price, 'Organizational Dynamics', *Amacom*, Summer 1977.
4. Boerlijst, 'Career Development and Career Guidance', in P. Drenth, H. Thierry, P. Willems, and C. de Wolff (eds) *Handbook of Work and Organizational Psychology*, John Wiley 1984.
5. Evans, P., and F. Bartolomé, op. cit.
6. Nicholson, N., and A. West, *Managerial Job Change: Men and women in transition* Cambridge University Press, 1988.
7. Mullins, L. J., *Management and Organizational Behaviour* (2nd ed.), Pitman, 1989.
8. Mitchell, T. R., 'Motivation: New Directions for Theory, Research and Practice', Academy of Management Review, Vol. 7, No. 1, January 1982.
9. Mullins, L. J., op. cit.
10. Locke, E. A., 'Towards a Theory of Task Motivation and Incentives', *Organizational Behaviour and Human Performance*, Vol. 3, 1968.
11. Goffee, R., and R. Scase, 'Are the Rewards Worth the Effort? Changing Managerial Values in the 1980s', *Personnel Review*, Vol. 15, No. 4, 1986.
12. Evans, P., and F. Bartolomé, op. cit.
13. Schein, E. H., *Career Dynamics: Matching individual and organizational needs*, Addison Wesley, 1978.
14. Brooklyn Derr, C., *Managing the New Careerists*, Josey Bass, 1986.
15. Sofer, C., *Men in Mid-Career*, Cambridge University Press, 1970.
16. Keen, P. G. W., 'Cognitive Style and Career Specialization' in J. van Maanen (ed), *Organizational Careers: Some new perspectives*, John Wiley, 1977.
17. Hudson, L., *Contrary Imaginations*, Methuen, 1966.
18. Witkin, H. A., D. R. Goodenough, 'Field Dependence and Interpersonal Behaviour', *Psychological Bulletin*, Vol. 84, No. 4, 1977.
19. Keen, P. G. W., op. cit.

20. Evans, P., and F. Bartolomé, op. cit.
21. Maccoby, M., *The Gamesman: The new corporate leader*, Secker and Warburg, 1977.
22. Storey, W. D., *Career Dimensions III*, GEC, 1976.

8
Career strategies in a changing world

8.1 Introduction

Career strategies in a changing world are likely to have to become much more proactive than they have been in the past. While accurate self-knowledge and assessment is the beginning of the process, it is not sufficient to stop there. The ability and willingness to anticipate and confront the changes outlined in Chapter 2 that form a context for career management are vital, as each of these major areas is evolving in its own right and in relation to others in the environment. The simple rhetorical question 'What am I here for?' is useful in that it forces managers to look inwards and outwards at the same time – at their own unique personalities and at changing scenarios. Perhaps the question may have been easy for some managers to answer, say, a few years ago, but for others, now the clarity may suddenly disappear with a change in organizational emphasis or refocusing. Indeed, one senior manager in a large financial institution said:

> I'm having to phase myself out of my current job. I don't know what I'll be doing next and it doesn't bother me now. There's so much change – I've given up worrying since I only had two days' notice about taking up my current post.

While there is no recipe for individual career planning and organizational career management, there *are* certain discernible pointers to key areas that managers need to grasp if they are to be successful in the future business environment. These continually appear, whether the starting point is macro- or national economic events, organizational policies and practices or individual behaviour. While this is not intended to be a comprehensive or definitive categorization, the most noticeable areas seem to be:

– global and cross-cultural awareness
– sensitivity to values – ethical, social and personal
– critical competences.

The career planning process does not stop here as managerial experiences, values and competences have to be built into a marketable career. Strategies then have to be identified that will encourage the most appropriate career path to be found.

8.2 Global and cross-cultural awareness

The necessity for future managers to take a global and cross-cultural perspective is being highlighted by the nature of world trade, the rapidity with which political and economic changes can occur and the resulting commercial pressures to adapt. An example of where all these have come together is in the new geography of Eastern Europe and the USSR, with the consequent and immediate appraisal of business opportunities, professional advice and joint ventures by those in the West. Indeed, some headhunters are already keeping a database of people who speak Russian and Eastern European languages, and those who provide management education and training are busily forging links in anticipation of future demands. As these new business partners come from the opposite side of the world, an appreciation of their countries' economics, lifestyles, product preferences and values is becoming extremely important. Of the top 20 world banks, 10 are Japanese. They in turn are investing heavily in European countries in anticipation of the single market. Increasingly they will look for the euromanager to run their European sales and marketing businesses and yet keep in close contact with Japan. Multinationals and newly merged businesses will also be on the lookout for them.

The euromanager

Who are these new euromanagers? A composite profile (the elements gleaned from the business press, publicity given to various reports and advertisements) would seem to suggest a specification that is currently difficult to meet. Recruitment consultancies are already setting up specialist units to capture this rare bird in the face of demographic and skills shortages.

First and foremost the euromanager is not to be confused with certain management career types.[1] Those with international experience gained through exporting or having worked abroad as an expatriate are not necessarily what is wanted, even though their experience *is* valuable. The reason for this is that in these situations these managers are more like participant observers. They never truly enter into the host culture because of the links with the organization back home and the short-term perspective produced by the length of stay. The euromanager, on the other hand, needs to be able to empathize with the nationals and have a sensitivity and respect for their culture and norms.

One such person was Pierre. Born in France, the son of a diplomat, he had lived in Switzerland and Germany. He obtained an MBA from a North American university and came to work in the UK as a consultant. He subsequently went to Italy as a marketing manager. He felt totally at ease moving around and did not consider this a hardship.

Second, a business degree and fluency in several languages, on their own, only provide a *framework* for communication. Managerial attitudes and practices vary, as do the way business deals are conducted and the terms and conditions that surround them. Therefore, experience of working in multinationals is an advantage. With the French, developing a social relationship is a very important preliminary, whereas the North Americans have a more legalistic attitude. Success as a euromanager requires for there to be a feeling of being at home with and flexible in the face of cultural differences, rather than judging them as inferior or acceptable from his or her own cultural perspective. If managers have a track record of having to enter new fields or environments, this will give an idea of how adaptable and able to learn they are.

Third, there is a need for an appreciation of other countries' relative strengths in relation to business requirements. Spain, for instance is attractive to the automotive industry because of its relatively skilled and medium-priced labour. France has able engineers and Germany is renowned for the efficiency of its production. In Continental education and training, there is a strong quantitative approach, especially in the economic and production fields, rather than a tendency to be merely judgemental as may happen in the UK. Technical and vocational training in France and Germany are more strongly valued and therefore receive greater support than they do here.

Fourth, there is the relation of work and private life, which differs among European countries. Spaniards are said to subordinate their working hours to their personal and social lives, making less of a rigid distinction between the two. By contrast, Germans are thought to be reluctant to work overtime, but still make very good use of their working day. In a cross-cultural study of 84 European high-flying executives at INSEAD, the international business school, internal career orientations (see Chapter 7) of the UK managers were stronger on the 'getting ahead' orientation compared to the French. The latter were more marked by leaning towards the 'getting balanced' orientation, as were the Germans. This may be a reflection of the fact that the French and Germans tend to expect to be less mobile within and between companies and develop strong regional and local loyalties.

Finally, notions of what it takes to be successful in a career differ across cultures, even when people are working for the same corporation. In a survey of 262 middle managers of 5 nationalities,[3] the Germans believed that the key characteristic was creativity, the British thought it was the right image and the French felt it was the ability to manage power relationships. Any euromanagers will need to be able to identify and be sensitive to these differences when operating in a foreign setting, as it will be by these norms that their contribution will be assessed. It is also worth noting that the corporate success model, underpinned by an appraisal system that may be designed from corporate headquarters, is likely to cause problems if nationalities are operating on their own cultural perspectives of career success. It is also likely to be met with further suspicion as a formal appraisal is seen as personal criticism in many European countries.

8.3 Sensitivity to values

Some areas that have received increasing prominence and which will affect managers' choices of and successes in their careers are the centrality of certain values to the individual and to the corporation. The ones that are continually surfacing are:

- business ethics
- the balance between work and personal life
- self-development

and these are now considered in turn.

Business ethics

Business ethics has now become a firmly established subject at many British business schools, perhaps reflecting an awareness of its importance in the business community with recent, high-profile court cases.

Organizations, for their part, are increasingly formulating mission statements as an anchor point for corporate strategy. These, such as the Johnson and Johnson credo, are of importance not only in guiding the day-to-day behaviour in organizations, but also in determining the response to and the outcome of corporate crises. For instance, products may be withdrawn for ethical or health reasons, costing the company millions of pounds; business operations in certain countries may be closed because of the political situation and certain business alliances may be discontinued.

The ethical stance of a company is increasingly being scrutinized by would-be recruits. They expect more than the platitude that the only responsibility of business is to make profits. In matters of pollution control, conflicts of interest, public and employee health and safety, destruction of natural resources, minority rights, consumer protection, fair commercial practice and insider dealing, the corporate reputation is at stake. Transgressors now receive more free publicity than before and are concerned at damage limitation. Public relations consultants are making it their business to be on hand to advise such organizations on how to ride these storms.

All this has implications for the senior managers' own careers as ethical considerations are threads that are likely to run through many aspects of executive decision making. At a second order level, a manager's staff must also accept these principles as, ultimately, their own boss's survival will depend on it, being accountable as he or she is for their subordinate's mistakes. It is now becoming a selling point for companies to publicize support for social, medical and environmental charities and to use their ethical and concerned stance as a marketing tool. Indeed, shared values are becoming critically important to organizations as they become global and decentralized and less subject to direct control.

Balancing work with private life

Maintaining a balance between the demands of corporate and private life is also on the management agenda. Chapter 7 covered this and showed not only the spillover effect but also the move against being 'taken over' by the employing organization. This trend to 'getting balanced' as a career orientation is also facilitated by an interest in the new organizational employment policies, which are offering more flexibility, and by the enabling technology (see Chapter 2). The general manager facing this situation has to generate ways of working 'smarter' rather than 'harder' to allow a committed work-force to develop.

Self-development

The opportunity for personal development has become an important issue for managers in their drive to stay employable rather than merely be employed. The rapid growth of distance learning to various levels of achievement (certificates, diplomas and MBAs) is continuing. People realize that to remain in work, existing skills must be topped up and new ones developed.

The organizational provision for open learning and the willingness to sponsor individuals with varying degrees of support (financial and leave of absence) is growing. It is being used as a powerful recruitment and retention tool, right from graduate to senior manager level. It is also a way of motivating plateaued managers.

8.4 Critical competences

The new manager may not only adopt different values but will have to maintain and acquire new competences. The following list is not intended to be comprehensive but it does indicate a range – some more suitable to some organizational cultures than others – in terms of relative importance and mix. The ones considered here are:

- flexibility
- learning facility
- generalist and specialist orientation and skills
- human resource and network management.

Flexibility

In a recent report[4] about 10 leading European companies' ways of being winners in the global markets of the 1990s 'the flexible manager' emerges as a key factor.

Because of the environmental changes outlined in Chapter 2, managers will be operating in a looser and, therefore, more ambiguous, organizational structure. They will also have less rigid boundaries. The ones that do exist will be created not so much by a given organizational structure but by the tasks organizations will carry out in their international role.

Geographical boundaries will not be emphasized as much as those relating to marketing areas. Crossdisciplinary and international teams will be formed and disbanded to tackle new ventures and problems. Skills in project management will therefore be vital and the number and frequency of bosses a manager may have will have implications for how careers are managed.

One caveat to all this is that there is a fine balance to be struck between flexibility and control: too much *flexibility* and the ideas within corporate missions, strategies and tactics become unworkable and the organization dissipates its energy; too much *control* and initiative becomes stifled and energy is lost through internal politics and the disruptive competition involved in guarding territories and reputations. These two opposing trends may be caricatured by examples of their extremes: the very young, hi-tech organization where formal responsibilities keep changing; the mature bureaucracy where structure and boundaries are difficult to change because they are internally connected to so many others.

Learning facility

As a second competence, this underpins the requirement for flexibility. To be able to respond to and manage change, the manager needs to be comfortable accepting rather than fighting it. Confidence, developed through being placed in new situations, grows as new strategies emerge for dealing with unfamiliar problems. How this is done depends not only on differing cognitive styles (see Chapter 7), but also on individual learning styles. One classification[5] is based on a study of managers from several functions:

- *theorists*: who like to learn by having a framework to see how parts of their experience fit together
- *pragmatists*: who learn by testing out the knowledge they have acquired and asking how it applies to their own situation
- *reflectors*: who prefer to consider all the angles and complexities of a situation and think about the interrelationships
- *activists*: who adopt 'learning by doing' as their motto – immersion in many different experiences and at a good pace is how they learn best.

Each type has different ways of absorbing information and learning about the world around them and profiles vary for different types of function. Some individuals may be strong on several styles, but others may develop a dominant one. To expand their range of learning styles, individuals can decide to place themselves in situations that they would normally avoid. For example, reflectors may volunteer to do more in-company presentations, which involves more 'thinking on your feet'. This would improve their confidence, activist-style.

The implications for managers are that they must not only be aware of how they learn best but that they can, if they desire, increase the range of situations and experiences from which they will learn by developing their learning styles. This itself will contribute to their flexibility.

The development of a learning facility within the individual cannot flourish unless the organizational culture permits it. This involves a celebration of success and an analysis of the reasons behind it and also an acknowledgement of and a constructive review of failure. This encourages the individual to take initiatives and supports them in taking considered risks. It means that managers have to be comfortable with differences and also see how they may be resolved. This attitude, to encourage the learning individuals who in turn make up the learning organization, begins at board level. Otherwise it will wither or be actively discouraged by individuals with an accountability for short-term objectives.

Generalist and specialist orientation and skills

For a third competence, this may sound contradictory. The point here is that managers could be of more use to their organizations if they had one or even two areas of expertise apart from being able to manage in a general sense. Not only would this keep them in a learning mode, but it would give them flexibility in a choice of career and opportunities to carve out new niches for themselves, as the examples in Chapter 6 show.

The possession of several areas of expert or functional competence prevents a narrow perspective being taken on problems. It also allows managers to build bridges with other colleagues working in task forces and to add to the networks to which managers belong. However, the ease with which these orientations can develop will depend on the organization's culture. If compartmentalization is adhered to, the learning opportunities to develop and apply these broader skills in new contexts will not be provided.

Human resource and network management

This fourth competence is human resource management attitudes and skills in the sense of being able to deal effectively with people and help to create or sustain a strong company culture.

Rather than being the sole province of the human resources department, it is another key area for managers to develop. This need follows from the trend to flatter organizational structures and less rigid boundaries between functions. Skills in obtaining cooperation and handling conflict, therefore, become critical where formal lines of authority and accountability may have become blurred over time. They may even have disappeared altogether in times of rapid change.

These same skills also apply in managing the networks outside and inside the organization. Relations with external stakeholders and the public, with suppliers and distributors of products or services will require harmonization, as organizations' activities increasingly come under scrutiny. Even if the new senior manager acquires the international awareness, sensitivity to values and critical competences outlined above, there is still the question of how to sequence and integrate all this to best advantage in a marketable career.

8.5 Building a marketable career

An interesting and speculative commentary on 'the best path to follow' to get to the top is based on a report[6] of a survey of 50 executives attending a conference on the structure and future of international corporations that took place in the USA.

First, an MBA programme will be needed to familiarize the future chief executive with the various forms of analysis and marketing tools in business and the behavioural sciences. Next, a spell in marketing or sales and some time spent overseas. Language skills at this stage should include Russian and Chinese to prepare for the new markets opening up. A general mastery of information technology and information management is important but especially in distribution as vast amounts of capital are locked up in these systems. Savings here would have substantial effects and improve competitive edge.

Although this outline is based on a commercial or industrial pattern, it is still useful for those in other sectors. Central and local government, healthcare, social work and legal and professional services are all having to become more marketing aware. Questions that their senior managers are now asking themselves are 'Who is my customer or client?' In the sectors just mentioned, there may be several, often with apparently irreconcilable objectives. Accountabilities are now being framed in such a way as to require a sensitivity to relevant indicators of operational performance and their management through the use of IT and accounting and financial reporting systems.

Whatever the skills, abilities and experience the executive acquires, visibility is still important – the manager must be seen to have displayed the required characteristics successfully. This needs to be brought to the attention of other senior managers and even chief executives, some of whom see spotting key people as an important part of their role in leading their organization. At the same time, visibility implies risk. For those prepared to take it, there are some ways to become noticed.

One ambitious junior manager used to send copies of relevant or novel articles that had impressed him to a director. At first, the director politely acknowledged receipt of the enclosed, then, if he met the junior manager, he might discuss it in passing. The point here is his name became known for showing some initiative and emerged from being just a face in the organizational crowd. Other ways that the same manager enhanced his reputation were by volunteering for presentations to senior management and by representing his work group in meetings within different parts of the organization.

In another enterprise, a manager used to write articles for trade journals and speak at conferences. This would be noted in the organization's newsletter, complete with picture. Visibility, therefore, enhances reputation both inside and outside the oganization and starts to create a situation where opportunities for individuals seem to appear without effort.

8.6 Individual strategies for career development

While not everyone will wish to or be able to tread the path to the CEO's office, there are some career strategies that individuals may adopt depending on the extremity of their environment and on the time they believe they have left to devote to a work career or to make new choices:

- survival
- adaptability
- growth.

The modes implied in the first and second of these are short- and medium-term options and, as such, will not be as productive in career development as the third. It should be said that the categories are based on the author's observations of managers rather than on substantial research. However, they relate to *real* examples and give an indication of the thinking behind the moves.

Survival strategies

These are aimed at maintaining rather than enhancing one's position. There is no real long-term orientation, only self-protection. The type of managers who use this may be, for example, functional specialists.

MOVING TO A SIMILAR JOB

When conditions are difficult or when their ambitions are thwarted, they will move to a similar function in a similar type of organization rather than have to adapt their skills to something totally new. When they accept a job they will probably look for an exit path so that they do not become trapped.

Michael was one such survivor. His skills were based in the personnel function: training, management development, manpower planning and career management. A career of over 20 years had been spent in IT companies or financial services organizations relying on IT. Each move brought a salary increase but now the peak had been reached. His attitude was to continue with this strategy, which had worked well in the past. There was no drive to become more adaptable. However, this attitude could be risky if a miscalculation occurred in the reading of the commercial environment as no allowance has been made for the need to learn new skills.

FOLLOWING THE BOSS

Another way of surviving is following in the footsteps of one's former boss. In this way, the same skills can be maintained and the boss does most of the adapting, providing a protective barrier around the subordinate. The latter then continues in the same mould as before. This only works if the manager is prepared to take the loyal, indispensable deputy role rather than have any personal and independent ambitions. It is also comforting to the sponsor who in a new situation can have a confidant.

The danger here is that the bosses may themselves become vulnerable or alter the mix of their protégés. From the point of view of the more junior manager, this strategy also has to take into account the risks of overdependence on one sponsor and the potential difficulty of building another career.

SCOURING INTERNAL INFORMATION

Mergers, acquisitions and divestments also test the skills of the survivor. He or she needs to be adept at reading the signs and judging the timing of the change. Assessing whether his or her particular function or skill will remain in high demand when the changes take place is critical here. This can only be done by keeping close to the internal networks and monitoring external sources of information carefully. These could be the business and sectoral press and other transmitters, which will provide the individual with the required information ahead of time. The networks will also yield news about job opportunities elsewhere and the reaction of competitors.

SCOURING EXTERNAL INFORMATION

A fourth survival strategy that is ongoing and demanding is to scour the appointments columns for information about targetted companies advertising there. Even if it is for jobs not immediately related to one's own skills, clues to their plans and operations may nevertheless be useful.

It is a way of identifying suitable openings that would logically follow, say, in a year, from the function or market niche they are currently trying to establish or develop. These can therefore be carefully targetted when the time is right. Keeping in touch with headhunters by passing on names will also stand the individual in good stead when the time comes for a move.

Adaptability

It goes beyond mere survival. Instead of keeping the same skills in action, a person who is adaptable will use them in different combinations and strengths, reactivate old ones or apply them in a different context. One method for doing this can be using each job as a stepping stone. In this way, the transition is not too great, is apparently seamless and the skill combinations can be readjusted.

Take, for instance, David who started as a salesman of electrical equipment with a multinational company and rose to become a sales manager. He then left for another multinational company making consumer and professional electrical goods. There he became a sales and marketing trainer. Within the same group he became a personnel and training manager of a division selling computers. He then left for the sales operation of another multinational of hi-tech equipment as head of human resources, finally being promoted to managing director.

The point here is that there is some consistency (employment with multinationals) and adaptability in that three core areas (sales, hi-tech products and human resources) have all been exploited in different sequences. Nevertheless, in each job this has been with a different emphasis to the point where real growth in experience and responsibility has taken place.

This adaptable mode also applies to professional careers in organizations. One view[7] is that the:

> professional and entrepreneurial career forms are better suited to innovative organizations operating in an uncertain and turbulent environment with high demands for change.

Professionals have transferable skills that can be directly applied in newer and/or larger contexts or as part of a multidisciplinary project team. The latter may be in sectors such as construction, property development, financial consortia, advising on mergers or acquisitions, special investigations and hi-tech to name but a few. In these instances:

> careers are produced by projects . . . and a key variable in success is reputation.[8]

Here, reputation is granted by other professionals and clients. Career success depends on performing well on the previous assignment. That is why consultants often say; 'You're only as good as your last job'. In fact, the adaptable mode allows room to manoeuvre and avoids taking on jobs without any credible means of exit.

Growth

The third broad strategy here is that of continual personal growth. What the individual is doing is actively gaining new skills, maybe while using the adaptable mode to stay in employment. At the same time, these new skills will open up new opportunities.

Personal growth can be achieved at work in two main ways: work experience and education and continuously reflecting on the knowledge gained from both.

WORK EXPERIENCE

Work experience can offer growth in a variety of ways (see Chapter 2). One management commentator[9] sees the,

> entrepreneurial career as the one in which growth occurs through the new value or organizational capacity [provided by the individual]

The 'key resource is the ability to create a product of service or value'. This is in contrast to the professional career where the resources are knowledge and reputation. Risks are greater with the entrepreneurial career than with others, but then so are the rewards. Under these circumstances personal growth for the careerist equals organizational growth.

If the entrepreneurial spirit cannot be satisfied or is restricted internally, there are plenty of options outside, as the trend to increasing numbers in self-employment continues (see Chapter 2). Sometimes these changes and new experiences lead to growth through self-understanding that cannot be achieved in the ways suggested in Chapter 7. For example, people may underestimate the importance of certain features in their lives or, having tested the water, may find that they have the wrong personality traits to operate in this entrepreneurial way.

Some of the most important qualities needed for the entrepreneurial career are said[10] to be: resilience, self-confidence, ruthlessness, persistence, efficiency, assertiveness, concern for quality, meeting deadlines, problem solving and the ability to think ahead. Undertaking contract work for one's employer, freelance consulting and developing hobbies into a business (such as wine exporting) are all possible options. A half-way house is that of franchising where new skills can be learned at the organization's expense. For instance, it is very much in the franchisor's interests to have managers who can at least read a balance sheet and set of accounts, understand the significance of business ratios and know which of these have particular significance for their operation. Mistakes with poorly selected or supported franchises can be costly for all concerned. Training in these areas is therefore a sound investment for both parties. Moreover, it enables a consistency in approach and reporting arrangements to be achieved straight away, thus ensuring a better chance of success.

The second main route to personal growth is education and training, again by a variety of methods outlined in Chapter 6. Banks now provide career development loans of £5000 that are interest-free for the first year, as more and more MBA and other students are paying their own way. While some are dependent on bank loans, others are taking out a second mortgage or may have a high-earning partner who will support them. They clearly see the qualification as an investment, bearing as they do the financial and opportunity costs involved. While some organizations distrust this trend to acquire an MBA and believe it just fuels a tendency for the newly qualified ones to leave (which in some cases it does), discouraging staff is the surest way to losing them anyway.

One caveat here – qualifications and the knowledge gained while acquiring them, like everything else, can become out of date. Continuous education and training has, therefore, to become the norm.

8.7 Conclusion

For survival in the 1990s, then, it is clear that possession of certain values and competences – many already discussed – will be vital. If business education as provided by an MBA and/or recognized by charter gives all people a grounding in the same basic disciplines, what will distinguish the star performer from the rest of the pack?

If, on the other hand, organizations so tailor their programmes and embed them in their own cultures, what transferability of skills and experience will there be?

Perhaps the answer lies in individuals developing their own unique career portfolio. This will contain general and specific roles, work experience, skills, values and behaviour. Development of this portfolio would produce a flexibility and responsiveness of their talents to meet organizational needs. This could, in part, be achieved by consideration of the examples in Chapter 6 relating to the position of generalists and multispecialists and the issues raised regarding turning them into line managers, for example. However, this portfolio has to be properly managed and maintained over the life of its owner. Much time and energy will have been invested in it and its value will change as the world changes, perhaps overnight. Therefore, it must be kept up to date, reviewed for its potential and marketed. The marketing need not be in the wider commercial sense, but through careful targetting and networking.

The role of the general manager, therefore, will be to encourage managers to invest in and develop their portfolios. Within them, several 'career jigsaws' may be in the process of completion at the same time: generalist versus specialist; functional versus organizational experience; national versus global responsibility, and so on.

It will thus be impossible for senior managers to be prescriptive about these portfolios. What they *can* do is provide a view about what they see in them and how parts of them could fit into the needs of their organization, if this is what their staff want. *With* their staff they can then help to create the new managerial careers that are opening up. In the process, they will most certainly discover much of value about their own careers, being an observer and facilitator to those of so many others.

Action questions

SENIOR MANAGERS

Can you identify any needs to change cross-cultural awareness, sensitivity to values and critical competences in your organization?
Are you making these known to your staff so that they can prepare and adapt themselves?

MANAGERS

Can you identify any career strategies that you have been adopting?
Are you a survivor, adapter or a growth person in career terms?
What has your career portfolio to offer your changing organization?

HUMAN RESOURCE SPECIALISTS

Are you encouraging your managers to build a marketable career?
Can you identify the survivors?
Is there anything you might do to help?

References

1. Golzen, G., 'Styling the Culture Sensitive Euromanager', *The Sunday Times*, Section E, 23 July 1990.
2. Brooklyn Derr, C., and A. Laurent, 'The Internal and External Careers: A theoretical and cross-cultural perspective', No. 87/24, *INSEAD*, Spring 1987.

3. 'The Cross-Cultural Puzzle of International Human Resource Management', *Human Resource Management*, Vol. xxv. No. 1, 1986.
4. Barham, K., J. Fraser, L. Heath, *Management for the Future: How leading international companies develop managers to achieve their vision*, Ashridge Management College and The Foundation for Management Education, 1988.
5. Honey, P., and A. Mumford, *Using Your Learning Styles*, Peter Honey, 1986.
6. Partridge, C., 'The Turn of the Shrewd', *Daily Telegraph Appointments*, 21 June 1990.
7. Moss Kanter, R., *When Giants Learn to Dance*, Simon and Schuster, 1989.
8. Moss Kanter, R., op. cit.
9. Moss Kanter, R., op. cit.
10. Saunders, P., *The Cranfield New Entrepreneur: Making your ideas work*, Cranfield, Sidgwick and Jackson, 1989.

Index